NEW DIRECTIONS FOR HIGHER EDUCATION

Martin Kramer
EDITOR-IN-CHIEF

Identifying and Preparing Academic Leaders

Sherry L. Hoppe
Bruce W. Speck
Austin Peay State University

EDITORS

Number 124, Winter 2003

JOSSEY-BASS
San Francisco

IDENTIFYING AND PREPARING ACADEMIC LEADERS
Sherry L. Hoppe, Bruce W. Speck (eds.)
New Directions for Higher Education, no. 124
Martin Kramer, Editor-in-Chief

Microfilm copies of issues and articles are available in 16mm and 35mm, as well as microfiche in 105mm, through University Microfilms Inc., 300 North Zeeb Road, Ann Arbor, Michigan 48106-1346.

NEW DIRECTIONS FOR HIGHER EDUCATION (ISSN 0271-0560, electronic ISSN 1536-0741) is part of The Jossey-Bass Higher and Adult Education Series and is published quarterly by Wiley Subscription Services, Inc., a Wiley company, at Jossey-Bass, 989 Market Street, San Francisco, California 94103-1741. Periodicals Postage Paid at San Francisco, California, and at additional mailing offices. POSTMASTER: Send address changes to New Directions for Higher Education, Jossey-Bass, 989 Market Street, San Francisco, California 94103-1741.

New Directions for Higher Education is indexed in Current Index to Journals in Education (ERIC); Higher Education Abstracts.

SUBSCRIPTIONS cost $80 for individuals and $160 for institutions, agencies, and libraries. See ordering information page at end of book.

EDITORIAL CORRESPONDENCE should be sent to the Editor-in-Chief, Martin Kramer, 2807 Shasta Road, Berkeley, California 94708-2011.

Cover photograph and random dot by Richard Blair/Color & Light © 1990.

www.josseybass.com

CONTENTS

EDITORS' NOTES

Charan, Drotter, and Noel (2001) join countless other leadership authors in noting that the demand for leadership greatly exceeds the supply. Corporations and universities alike are turning to search firms to fill leadership voids. More significant, the time in leadership positions—in business and in education—has decreased dramatically in the past decade. No longer do leaders stay in the same position for ten, twenty, or even thirty years. Leaders move frequently, either for advancement or escape from an intolerable situation. Those seeking leaders for critical academic roles are often unable to determine whether a person is leaving a position because of success or because of failure. Finding the most qualified person with the greatest potential for making a difference is thus often little more than the roll of the dice. This volume, while not promising to correct the deficiencies of the current system (or lack thereof), may provide some insight about how to prepare individuals in the academy to assume leadership roles as department chairs, deans, academic vice presidents, provosts, and presidents. The chapters explore how to identify those with leadership potential, nurture future academic leaders, discover both traditional and nontraditional paths to academic leadership positions, develop diverse ways to prepare for leadership roles, and support effective leadership practices. Our goal is to provide a basic framework for those seeking academic leadership roles and for those searching for future leaders.

In Chapter One, Sherry Hoppe identifies desirable leadership characteristics and suggests ways to assess and nurture those attributes in potential academic leaders.

Patricia Land avows in Chapter Two that the varied and complex responsibilities of today's academic leaders require skills that can be garnered as easily in student affairs or other nonacademic roles as in the traditional success path beginning with faculty and moving to department chair.

In Chapter Three, Gary Filan and Alan Seagren cite the need for training for complex leadership roles in higher education and describes one exemplary training program.

Shirley Raines and Martha Squires Alberg make the case in Chapter Four that academics need opportunities to learn how to become effective administrators and describe those opportunities.

Next, Bruce Speck asserts his belief in Chapter Five that doctoral programs should go beyond preparing faculty for scholarship in their discipline and engage them in multidimensional roles of the academy.

In Chapter Six, Susan Whealler Johnston analyzes the role of shared governance in effective administration of academic affairs.

Charles Jenkins then delineates in Chapter Seven major constitutional and statutory provisions that affect academic administrators' decisions and actions and provides an overview of other legal considerations.

In Chapter Eight, Oscar Page argues that promoting diversity in academic leadership is not only right but essential in modeling servant leadership.

Christina Murphy focuses in Chapter Nine on how to motivate and reward academic leaders, both intrinsically and extrinsically.

Daryl Gilley ends the volume by illustrating an effective bedside manner for a bevy of characters in higher education's culture in a light-hearted yet insightful way, emphasizing interpersonal aspects of communication.

Sherry L. Hoppe
Bruce W. Speck
Editors

Reference

Charan, R., Drotter, S., and Noel, J. *The Leadership Pipeline: How to Build the Leadership-Powered Company*. San Francisco: Jossey-Bass, 2001.

SHERRY L. HOPPE *is president of Austin Peay State University in Clarksville, Tennessee.*

BRUCE W. SPECK *is professor of English and vice president for academic affairs at Austin Peay State University in Clarksville, Tennessee.*

1

Selecting and nurturing academic leaders requires identifying effective leadership characteristics and providing experiences for potential candidates that both test and develop them.

Identifying and Nurturing Potential Academic Leaders

Sherry L. Hoppe

In higher education, the academic leadership pipeline has historically flowed from a department chair rotational system, with little or no succession planning. Until recently, senior faculty willing to do their share of administrative work simply took a turn as department chair and then returned (relieved and often disillusioned) to their tenured professorial role. Today, increasing numbers are unwilling to take their turn, and too few are eager to volunteer for administrative roles. Why is this so often the case? Smith (1996) believes that "a person who doesn't feel the thrill of challenge is not a potential leader" (p. 30). I think academic leadership avoidance is more complex than that. The role conflicts involved in balancing creativity and autonomy with bureaucracy (Davenport, 2001) likely contribute to the reticence to assume academic leadership roles. In addition, considering the pittance that department chairs receive for their work, one wonders why anyone would aspire to that role. Fortunately, other incentives do exist, such as the intrinsic reward of service to the department or the potential for the role to be the entry point for a future deanship or vice presidency. Even so, Davenport (2001) notes, "For many, the power, prestige and increased income that often accompany managerial roles are not worth the trade-offs" (p. 57).

With a move away from rotational chairs and a reluctance to tackle the conflicting responsibilities inherent in the lower levels of academic leadership, how can those at the top of the pipeline identify faculty who have the ability and desire to move through the ranks? What characteristics will increase the probability of willingness, commitment, and perseverance?

How does one find those who have the integrity, values, and fortitude needed for making the right decisions for the right reasons? Once identified, how can potential academic leaders be nurtured and encouraged and developed? What experiences would be helpful to budding academic administrators? These are the questions this chapter examines.

Characteristics of Effective Academic Leaders

Identifying the characteristics of leadership takes only a limited effort, since the literature is replete with discussion of the attributes of successful leaders (Allen, 1980; Autry, 1991; Bennis, 1989a; Byham, 1982; Conger and Benjamin, 1999; Goleman, 1998; Hayes, 1980; Kouzes and Posner, 1993; Maccoby, 1981; McCauley, Moxley, and Velsor, 1998; Sonnenberg, 1993). At the top of the list in most studies is honesty (Kouzes and Posner, 1990). Followers want leaders they believe will be truthful, forthright, and trustworthy in their dealings with employees (Bennis, 1989b; Lee and King, 2001; Sonnenberg, 1993). Other commonly cited characteristics are integrity, credibility, fairness, high energy level, and perseverance (Byham, 1982; Bennis, 1989a, 1989b; Geneen, 1984; Kouzes and Posner, 1989; Kroc, 1977; Peters, 1987). Effective leaders demonstrate a strong goal orientation (Waitley, 1983), willingness to take risks (Deal and Kennedy, 1982; Whitney and Packer, 2002), good communication skills (McConkey, 1989; Waitley, 1983), and objective decision making (McConkey, 1989; Peters and Waterman, 1982; Ryan and Oestreich, 1991). They have the ability to adapt (Peters and Waterman, 1982; Waitley, 1983) and a desire to serve (Geneen, 1984). Many possess humility, some are creative, most are open; virtually all are dedicated and committed to the importance of what they are doing (Bennis, 1989a, 1989b; McConkey, 1989). The best ones have the capacity to tolerate the idiosyncrasies and weaknesses of others (Ryan and Oestreich, 1991).

Noticeably missing from this list is intelligence. Although some might argue that a high level of intelligence is essential for leaders, I purport that other competencies are more crucial. However, a leader does need enough intelligence to make decisions based on rational and objective reasoning. Reasoning and reflection, nevertheless, do not require the ability to do quantum physics.

In their efforts to identify how leadership affects not only the progress but also the development and survival of organizations, Bennis and Nanus (1985) interviewed ninety leaders, including sixty successful CEOs and thirty public sector heads. They concluded, "Leadership is like the Abominable Snowman, whose footprints are everywhere but who is nowhere to be seen" (p. 20). While recognizing that numerous common traits exist, Bennis and Nanus (1985) were nonplussed when they found very successful leaders who did not demonstrate all or even most of the identified characteristics. "They were right-brained and left-brained, tall and short, fat and thin, articulate and inarticulate, assertive and retiring, dressed for success and dressed for failure, participative and autocratic" (pp. 25–26). Despite the many commonly shared attributes, the researchers concluded, "There were more variations than themes. Even their managerial styles were restlessly different" (Bennis and Nanus, 1985, p. 26). For the authors, who were "interested in patterns, in underlying themes," the leaders interviewed were "frustratingly unruly" (p. 26).

Not to be deterred, Bennis and Nanus (1985) "vigilantly trolled these disparate powers for uniformities," looking for "kernels of truth about leadership—the marrow, if you will, of leadership behavior" (p. 26). What they found were four distinctly different strategies or competencies (pp. 26–27):

- "Attention through vision"—creating a focus or agenda based on a vision of the future
- "Meaning through communication"—with or without words, the ability to get people to adopt shared values and common goals
- "Trust through positioning"—consistency in accountability, predictability, and reliability of the mission or vision
- "The deployment of self through positive self-regard"—recognizing strengths and compensating for weaknesses; nurturing of skills with discipline

Respecting the research and conclusions of Bennis and Nanus (1985), those searching for potential academic leaders might find examples of intuitive identification as instructive as formal investigation of leadership characteristics or competencies. Harold Geneen, who served for seventeen years as the head of International Telephone and Telegraph Company, was a master at zeroing in on individuals with leadership potential. He himself was noted for his high energy level, natural enthusiasm, and quick mind. He liked his work, he worked hard, and he set a clear example for those who worked with him (Moscow, 1984). Undoubtedly, these traits would be a good place to start in looking for academic leaders. Geneen was quick to note that he did not want geniuses who were so intelligent they could not work with others. Instead, what he looked for were people who were capable, experienced, and motivated—people who wanted to make something of themselves and were not afraid to work hard for what they wanted. In short, he wanted people who shared his enthusiasm for work (Geneen, 1984).

While accepting the attributes discussed in the preceding paragraphs as desirable and even necessary, my experience indicates the most critical factor to look for in aspiring academic leaders is fortitude: the will to make the right decisions for the right reasons. Unfortunately, some faculty who move into leadership roles are unable to make the right (and often tough) decisions because they are too tied to their faculty colleagues and to commonly revered privileges of the academy. For example, the role of an academic department chair requires a faculty member to balance a tightly held commitment to faculty freedom and loyalties with the need to hold a broader view of the university, its budgetary constraints, and its obligations to the whole. Many faculty cannot distance themselves enough from their faculty myopia to see the big picture and to make decisions that serve the university rather than just the faculty. As a faculty member moves through the academic pipeline, the distancing becomes increasingly critical.

Caution must be exercised in avoiding the Peter Principle. Faculty members who are capable, experienced, and motivated in the classroom do not necessarily make capable (or even happy) administrators. Bennis (1989b), himself a former university president, postulates that experience at one level may well instill "certain principles and guidelines to action that were antithetical to the pneumatic beat" (p. 9) of new situations and crises an academic administrator may face in moving up the hierarchy. Although he was describing the movement of a dean to a president, the principle is applicable at all levels, and it reinforces the idea that a willingness to accept and embrace change may be the highest attribute for successful administrators.

Avoiding the Wrong Selection of Academic Leaders

Knowing what to avoid is just as important, if not more so, than knowing what to look for in potential leaders. A word of caution: just because someone wants to be a department chair or dean does not mean he or she will be effective in a leadership role. Nor does the best teacher necessarily make the best academic leader any more than the best violinist automatically makes the best conductor (Smith, 1996). An *Industry Week* article (Verespej, 1990) and a story of paradox (Harvey, 1988) provide clues that can be adapted to the academic environment to suggest those who should be avoided in the selection of academic leaders:

- Faculty who cannot move from colleague to leader (Maccoby, 1981)
- Faculty who manage by agreement. This could also be described as the "Abilene Paradox," a simple yet complex principle illustrated by the story of a family who takes a fifty-three-mile trip to Abilene, Texas, on a 104 degree day in an un-air-conditioned 1958 Buick on dusty dirt roads— despite the fact that none of them really wants to go. How could such a thing happen? It is rather simple: each thought the others wanted to go and thus refrained from saying what he or she really thought. It was only some four hours and 106 miles later that they admitted to one another (rather angrily) that they had all done just the opposite of what they had wanted to do. Watergate was another prime example of a group going down a road to an undesirable destination not because they wholeheartedly agreed on the mission but because they failed to express their reservations (Harvey, 1988).

- Faculty who are insensitive, aloof, or inflexible (Maccoby, 1981)
- Faculty who are unable to handle a crisis or performance problem (Maccoby, 1981)
- Faculty who fail to understand the internal and external environment (Maccoby, 1981)
- Faculty who do not know how to handle power (Maccoby, 1981)

This last flaw can be fatal for an academic administrator. Academic administrators at all levels (including presidents) must recognize they have only limited power regardless of their titles. In fact, the only true authority resides in the power of policy and the power of persuasion. Shared governance, combined with a litigious society that challenges most forms of authority and decision making, severely limits an administrator's effectiveness if it is not based on policy or persuasion. Collaboration, consistency in openness and full disclosure, and the ability to communicate a shared vision form the only legitimate basis of power in the academy. As in the military, titles do not guarantee real power, which is little more than the capacity to influence and inspire (Powell, 2001).

One last word of caution: recognize the value in a "constructive spirit of discontent" (Smith, 1996, p. 30). Smith differentiates between being critical and being constructively discontent:

> If somebody says, "There's got to be a better way to do this," I see if there's leadership potential by asking, "Have you ever thought about what that better way might be?" If he says no, he is being critical, not constructive. But if he says yes, he's challenged by a constructive spirit of discontent. That's the unscratchable itch. It is always in the leader [p. 30].

The Testing Ground: Finding Potential Academic Leaders

Thus far I have discussed the common characteristics of successful leaders and some attributes to avoid in the quest for potential leaders. Knowing what we want in leaders and what we do not want, how do we find those who have the potential and will to serve in academic administrative roles?

McCauley, Moxley, and Velsor (1998) identify assessment as step one of the leadership identification and development process. Reporting on the success of the Center for Creative Leadership, they suggest two methods: 360-degree feedback and the feedback-intensive program. Both enhance self-awareness and describe an individual's leadership skills and behaviors. The feedback-intensive program goes a step further, helping the person understand his or her needs, preferences, and values. These types of formal assessment are likely very helpful, but many institutions may lack the time or resources to use such tools. In the absence of such formal assessments, the search for potential academic leaders must take more intuitive (Geneen's method) or experience-based approaches.

Ohlott (1998) discusses the importance of developmental job assignments in identifying those who have the potential to move beyond the faculty role. These job assignments can be responsibilities added to an existing job (such as working on a short-term project or coordinating mentors), a piece of a job (such as dealing with a difficult employee or compiling information to use in schedule assignments), or an entire job (such as redesigning a system). In the academic world, it might also be chairing an accreditation self-study or taking a leadership role in developing an on-line program. For an extended test of leadership capability and performance, interim administrative assignments for up to a year serve as a fertile ground for testing and developing leaders.

A job assignment takes on a developmental role when it

> stretches people, pushes them out of their comfort zones, and requires them to think and act differently. It may involve roles that are not well defined, and it usually contains some elements that are new to the person. These assignments place people in a challenging situation full of problems to solve, dilemmas to resolve, obstacles to overcome, and choices to make under conditions of risk and uncertainty [Ohlott, 1998, p. 130].

The new assignments provide an opportunity to assess strengths or deficiencies, creativity, and tolerance for ambiguity. They can also be a test of decision making, conflict resolution, and interpersonal skills.

Developmental experiences are testing grounds for seeing how aspiring or potential academic administrators react to responsibilities that require them to juggle faculty desires and needs, student needs, and administration mandates. Balancing competing needs inevitably results in criticism from those who perceive their needs have been given insufficient weight or influence. Decision making for the good of the whole over the desire or need of one individual or group is a requisite yet difficult leadership action. Colin Powell (2001) provides some applicable and discerning lessons in his leadership primer:

> Good leadership involves responsibility to the welfare of the group, which means that some people will get angry at your actions and decisions. It's inevitable, if you're honorable. Trying to get everyone to like you is a sign of mediocrity: you'll avoid the tough decisions, you'll avoid confronting the people who need to be confronted, and you'll avoid offering differential rewards based on differential performance because some people might get upset. Ironically, by procrastinating on the difficult choices, by trying not to get anyone mad, and by treating everyone equally 'nicely' regardless of their contributions, you'll simply ensure that the only people you'll wind up angering are the most creative and productive people in the organization [slide 2].

Putting aspiring administrators in positions where they must demonstrate their willingness to make decisions is thus a good testing ground.

Within the developmental experiences and job assignments discussed above, specific practice or familiarity in the following areas would be beneficial to future academic leaders:

- Budget analysis and development (this could be project based, such as in grant development)
- Program development (current department chairs or deans could assign primary responsibility for new academic programs or curriculum revision to potential leaders)
- Schedule analysis or work-load review
- Policy analysis or development (such as providing leadership to review existing posttenure review policies)
- Internal coordination of externally based initiatives (such as chairing an internal United Way campaign)
- External representation of the university on special committees or boards (such as the chamber of commerce)
- Opportunity to visit or benchmark other institutions as the basis for planning changes within the department
- Skill-based training in areas such as budgeting, curriculum development, or assessment (this could be individual or group based)

Nurturing New Academic Leaders

Supporting potential academic leaders as they face the disequilibrium of new experiences is critical. Forced to make hard decisions that affect colleagues, inexperienced academic leaders often need to talk through their conflicts. They also may need reassuring when they begin "to question the adequacy of their skills, frameworks, and approaches" (Velsor, McCauley, and Moxley, 1998, p. 11). They may need assistance in recognizing that comfort zones inhibit growth and effectiveness (McCauley, Moxley, and Velsor, 1998). Challenging experiences can overwhelm or open one up for learning—those nurturing new leaders must confirm and reinforce positive steps toward independence and organizational viewpoints. Supporters, according to Velsor, McCauley, and Moxley (1998), should "listen to stories of struggle, identify with the challenges, suggest strategies for coping, reassure in times of doubt, inspire renewed effort, celebrate even the smallest accomplishments, and cheer from the sidelines" (p. 16). Peers, former bosses, and current bosses can all participate in the support network. Organizational norms and procedures can also be a source of structure and support (Velsor, McCauley, and Moxley, 1998).

Motivation to learn and grow needs nurturing. "Support helps engender a sense of self-efficacy about learning, a belief that one can learn, grow and change. The higher their self-efficacy, the more effort people exert to master challenges, and the more they persevere in difficult situations" (McCauley, Moxley, and Velsor, 1998, p. 16). Inexperienced academic administrators need to know that mistakes are acceptable and that open examination of those mistakes is a step toward growth. They also need to have developmental experiences in data-based decision making. Many faculty assume department head roles, and some even rise to the level of dean or vice president without ever learning how to build a schedule or make faculty teaching assignments. They are not taught to review student credit hour production by individual and by discipline, analyze faculty productivity, or manage class enrollments (monitoring cancelled sections, closed sections, and underenrolled sections). Many have never heard of a facilities utilization report, which can be instrumental in meeting student needs and maximizing resources. All of these data-driven analyses should be taught through mentoring or work sessions conducted by seasoned administrators. Aspiring administrators would do well to heed the advice of General Colin Powell (2001): "Never neglect details. . . . Pay attention to details."

Conclusion

Identifying, nurturing, and supporting potential leaders are critical components in maintaining a pipeline for continuity and infusion of new pools in academy administration. Higher education institutions that prepare for the future will have an identification strategy and developmental plan that not only provides for the next generation of leaders but also ensures that they have the experiences and skills necessary for success. The mobility of faculty complicates such planning, but careful identification and nurturing will keep the pipeline flowing. From the initial entry into the pipeline of academic leadership to the highest levels of vice president, provost, or even president, future leaders should be made fully aware of the responsibilities and accountability required of leaders.

Powell (2001) astutely sums up the essence of such responsibility and accountability: "Command is lonely. Harry Truman was right. Whether you're a CEO or the temporary head of a project team, the buck stops here. You can encourage participative management and bottom-up employee involvement, but ultimately the essence of leadership is the willingness to make the tough, unambiguous choices that will have an impact on the fate of the organization. I've seen too many non-leaders flinch from this responsibility. Even as you create an informal, open, collaborative corporate culture, prepare to be lonely" (slide 9).

With such a dismal warning, why would anyone want to be a leader, especially an academic leader? Bennis (1989a) believes the dearth of leaders can be attributed to the traditional spirit of American individualism, which translates into self first and others last. Add to this environment the relentless scrutiny and criticism of public servants, and the motivation to serve in a leadership role diminishes further. Today's culture supports the premise that the demands and negativism are not worth the sacrifice. How, then, can we get individuals with ability and integrity to seek leadership positions? I believe it is only through setting an example that builds values.

If faculty and rising administrators know what an institution stands for, they will likely be more willing to assume leadership roles. If leaders at the top of the institution demonstrate consistent values over a long period of time, others will share those values and will be motivated to pay the price of academic leadership. Inspiring others to share the vision is perhaps the most critical aspect in attracting and nurturing new leaders. Commitment to making a difference in the lives of others is the ultimate motivation.

References

Allen, F. "Bosses List Main Strengths, Flaws Determining Potential of Managers." *Wall Street Journal,* Nov. 14, 1980, p. 33.

Autry, J. A. *Love and Profit: The Art of Caring Leadership.* New York: Morrow, 1991.

Bennis W. *On Becoming a Leader.* Reading, Mass.: Addison-Wesley, 1989a.

Bennis, W. *Why Leaders Can't Lead.* San Francisco: Jossey-Bass, 1989b.

Bennis, W., and Nanus, B. *Leaders: The Strategies for Taking Charge.* New York: HarperCollins, 1985.

Bennis, W., Spreitzer, G. M., and Cummings, T. G. (eds.). *The Future of Leadership: Today's Top Leadership Thinkers Speak to Tomorrow's Leaders.* San Francisco: Jossey-Bass, 2001.

Byham, W. C. *Dimensions of Managerial Competence.* Bridgeville, Pa.: Development Dimensions International, 1982.

Charan, R., Drotter, S., and Noel, J. *The Leadership Pipeline: How to Build the Leadership-Powered Company.* San Francisco: Jossey-Bass, 2001.

Conger, J., and Benjamin, B. *Building Leaders: How Successful Companies Develop the Next Generation.* San Francisco: Jossey-Bass, 1999.

Davenport, T. "Knowledge Work and the Future of Management." In W. Bennis, G. M. Speitzer, and T. G. Cummings (eds.), *The Future of Leadership: Today's Top Leadership Thinkers Speak to Tomorrow's Leaders.* San Francisco: Jossey-Bass, 2001.

Deal, T. E., and Kennedy, A. A. *Corporate Cultures: The Rites and Rituals of Corporate Life.* Reading, Mass.: Addison-Wesley, 1982.

Geneen, H. *Managing.* New York: Doubleday, 1984.

Goleman, D. "What Makes a Leader?" *Harvard Business Review,* 1998, 76(6), 93–102.

Harvey, J. *The Abilene Paradox.* San Francisco: Jossey-Bass, 1988.

Hayes, J. L. "A Model of the Successful Manager." *American Schools and Universities,* 1980, 52, 14–16.

Kouzes, J. M., and Posner, B. Z. "The Credibility Factor: What People Expect of Leaders." *WKKF International Journal,* Fall–Winter 1990, pp. 26–29.

Kouzes, J. M., and Posner, B. Z. *Credibility: How Leaders Gain and Lose It, Why People Demand It.* San Francisco: Jossey-Bass, 1993.

Kroc, R. *Grinding It Out.* New York: McGraw-Hill, 1977.

Lee, R. J., and King, S. N. *Discovering the Leader in You.* San Francisco: Jossey-Bass, 2001.

Maccoby, M. *The Leader.* New York: Simon & Schuster, 1981.

McCauley, C. D., Moxley, R. S., and Velsor, E. V. (eds.). *The Center for Creative Leadership Handbook of Leadership Development.* San Francisco: Jossey-Bass, and Greensboro, N.C.: Center for Creative Leadership, 1998.

McConkey, D. D. "Are You an Administrator, a Manager, or a Leader?" *Business Horizons,* 1989, 32(5), 15–21.

Moscow, A. "Introduction." In H. Geneen, *Managing.* New York: Doubleday, 1984.

Ohlott, P. "Job Assignments." In C. D. McCauley, R. S. Moxley, and E. V. Velsor (eds.), *The Center for Creative Leadership Handbook of Leadership Development.* San Francisco: Jossey-Bass and Greensboro: Center for Creative Leadership, 1998.

Peters, T. *Thriving on Chaos.* New York: Knopf, 1987.

Peters, T., and Waterman, Jr., R. H. *In Search of Excellence.* New York: HarperCollins, 1982.

Powell, C. *A Leadership Primer.* Washington, D.C.: U.S. Department of the Army, 2001. [http://mba.tuck.dartmouth.edu/pages/club/afa/powell_primer.ppt].

Ryan, K. D., and Oestreich, D. K. *Driving Fear Out of the Workplace: Creating the High-Trust, High-Performance Organization.* (2nd ed.) San Francisco: Jossey-Bass, 1991.

Smith, F. "Leadership Qualities: Ten Ways to Identify a Promising Person." *Leadership Journal,* 1996, 17(4), 30. [http://www.nsba.org/sbot/toolkit/LeadQual.html].

Sonnenberg, F. K. "Trust Me, Trust Me Not." *Industry Week,* Aug. 16, 1993, pp. 22–26.

Velsor, E. V., McCauley, C. D., and Moxley, R. S. "Our View of Leadership Development." In C. D. McCauley, R. S. Moxley, and E. V. Velsor (eds.), *The Center for Creative Leadership Handbook of Leadership Development.* San Francisco: Jossey-Bass and Greensboro: Center for Creative Leadership, 1998.

Verespej, M. A. "Why Managers Fail: Visible Flaws Go Uncorrected." *Industry Week,* 1990, 42(1), 239.

Waitley, D. *Seeds of Greatness.* Old Tappan, N. J.: Fleming H. Revell, 1983.

Whitney, J. O., and Packer, T. *Power Plays.* New York: Simon & Schuster, 2002.

SHERRY L. HOPPE is president of Austin Peay State University in Clarksville, Tennessee.

2

Evolutionary paths for faculty are no longer sacred routes to chief academic officer roles.

From the Other Side of the Academy to Academic Leadership Roles: Crossing the Great Divide

Patricia C. Land

Few, if any, colleges or universities advertise career planning sessions for those who someday hope to become a chief academic officer (CAO) in higher education. Classroom teachers may desire to move into a principal's position even as they are preparing to teach, but it is unlikely that anyone ever dreams of growing up and taking the helm over curricula and college faculty. Thus, even though deans, department heads, and long-term faculty are those most likely to consider a step up into academic administration, it is generally an evolutionary process rather than a definitive career ladder aspiration held during their years as college students themselves. Most do not prepare for the position as part of graduate course work, since doctoral programs preparing faculty are generally limited to discipline-specific topics rather than academic administrative issues. (See Chapter Five for more on this topic.)

Even if doctoral programs included training in academic administration, adapting that training to individual institutions takes additional skills. Every campus functions differently, and every CAO's role generally varies with the style and goals of the president, as well as with the shared governance proclivity of the faculty. Job effectiveness depends on the CAO's ability to understand and learn the role behaviors peculiar to that institution (Mech, 1997).

The lack of preparation, combined with adaptability requirements and other demands, has caused the pool of potential academic leaders to decline in recent years. All colleges face turnover in leadership positions, but particularly dramatic numbers of potential retirements are being projected in community colleges, where nationwide hiring in the 1960s due to system growth is now producing large numbers of faculty and administrators ready to end or change their careers. Many community college academic officers intend to leave their current positions within five to ten years, whether to seek a presidency or because of job stress or other reasons (Murray and Murray, 2000). Although the situation is not as precipitous in universities, the number of vacancies in the next five to ten years will create significant voids in academic leadership positions unless the applicant pool is broadened. To ensure that colleges and universities are adequately prepared for the future, it is imperative that not only faculty but also talented leaders outside academics be encouraged to consider "crossing the great divide" to invest in the academic administrative future of the academy. This can increase the pool of potential academic administrators and also help meet the needs of the expanding role of academic leadership.

Historically, the CAO has been internally focused, working with faculty to ensure a quality academic program. However, leadership in the academy will increasingly require new skills, as academic vice presidents and provosts are forced to juggle internal duties and external demands for accountability. In addition to traditional job requirements, diverse skills, including leadership in information and educational technologies, institutional accountability, and learner assessment, will be demanded of new types of leaders (Bragg, 2000).

With these changing requirements, college and university officials must address the following areas:

- Alternative career paths to academic affairs
- How to identify future leaders from other administrative areas
- What strategies to implement to foster diversity in academic leadership

Alternative Career Paths for Academic Affairs

If a standard path were to be described for the CAO, it would typically involve starting as faculty and then moving to department head or dean before the appointment to vice president or provost. Cejda, McKenney, and Burley (2001) documented this reality when they looked for common entry positions for two-year-college CAOs and found that serving in a faculty position was the starting point for a majority of executive officers. Although they were unable to find a "single, normative job ladder" (p. 37) leading to appointment as a CAO, they argue that "progressive administrative positions" (p. 37) are key to preparing for a CAO position. Thus, for those who wish to increase their chance of becoming a CAO, the most likely place to begin is in the classroom. Most candidates have over ten years of teaching experience and have held at least three increasingly responsible positions within the college (Cejda, McKenney, and Burley, 2001).

Twombly (1988) studied administrative labor markets to determine whether specific career lines or paths existed within two-year colleges. He discovered that faculty and other academics often found career mobility by taking on additional responsibilities as a means to move up the career ladder, although other career paths did exist, including administrative deans or other nonacademic positions. Whether occupying a faculty position or one in a multitude of other areas across the college or university, such a willingness to participate in cross-functional committees is invaluable. Learning about the academic side of the house *is* possible even if one works across the tracks.

Because of the increasingly collaborative approach in executive leadership roles in universities, nonstandard paths to academic leadership may become more common at all levels but likely most often in community colleges. Twombly (1988) found that the likelihood of transition from a nontraditional career path into a CAO position was much greater in the two-year college because of the relative newness of the institution. Interestingly, community college CAOs frequently had been employed at a university prior to moving to a two-year college. As many as 40 percent of the community college CAOs studied had held at least one position in a four-year college (Twombly, 1988). Twombly (1988) concluded that administrative experience, not a particular position (that is, faculty status), was a significant factor in evaluating a career path.

Despite their reluctance, universities must face the need to identify and groom nontraditional candidates because the dearth of academic leaders falls to them as well as to two-year colleges. Mech's study (1997) of academic officers showed that smaller four-year institutions would find it difficult to be competitive in recruiting experienced candidates and therefore should prepare themselves to select their academic leaders from among candidates with less experience in pure academic areas. With fewer and fewer faculty willing to move into leadership roles, larger universities may also be forced to look outside the classroom for CAO candidates. Faculty may be willing to do their turn as department chairs, but moving to progressively responsible and demanding roles of academic leadership is not attractive when compared to teaching.

How to Identify Future Leaders from Other Administrative Disciplines

Perhaps this section should be rephrased as "skills that are needed for an effective CAO and where they can be found."

Many believe that the role of the CAO is unlike that of any other campus executive member. That is debatable and is discussed below. Regardless, few would argue with Mech (1997) when he stated, "The managerial behavior that is demanded of a successful department head is apt to be different from that of an effective CAO" (p. 284).

Although Mech (1997) found that the size of the institution ultimately influenced the scope of the CAO's authority, the variety of roles that an academic officer must assume can be overwhelming to a novice administrator. In smaller colleges, the span of control can be so large that an administrator can conceivably have little direct knowledge of all the functions he or she would be asked to supervise. Therefore, it is not unreasonable to assume that both administrative and student service personnel can be tapped to serve as future academic officers.

An academic leader should be able to direct environmental scanning of the college's service area to determine what academic programs are needed. This strategy places the CAO in contact with external constituencies and requires an understanding of community growth and economic development issues. A background in advancement, strategic planning, institutional research, or enrollment management would be helpful in fulfilling these needs.

The CAO must have strong interpersonal skills to bridge communications between faculty and other university administrators. He or she may frequently be required to assume the role of a mediator, using relationships to create harmony among various campus constituencies. For this reason, team-building skills become extremely important. These skills are especially critical in working with faculty. As an executive officer, the CAO must promote the college's mission or operational strategies by representing the president with the faculty, using skills that administrators elsewhere in the university also possess (Anderson, 1997). Mediation and team-building skills are often evident in student affairs leaders, and thus some from this group are beginning to cross the great divide that has historically existed between academic affairs and student services. Student service administrators bring to the management team the passion for education that is requisite to academic administration. They also have firsthand knowledge of how learning environments can enable diverse populations to succeed. For these reasons, student service officers' ability to transform student success into program planning can be a valuable asset to the leadership team. Likewise, because education has become accessible to more people than ever before, the ability to work with culturally diverse people, both faculty and students, will be a requirement for academic administrators (Townsend and Bassoppo-Moyo, 1997). Typically, student affairs officers are well grounded in this area and bring needed expertise to a CAO role.

As they attempt to mentor and develop the student population, college and university student affairs leaders usually display strong ethical values and personal integrity. Their experience and leadership by example in "safety, tolerance, respect for law . . . democracy, confidentiality . . . *and* teamwork" (Thomas, 2002, p. 66) is invaluable to academic administration. Those identified traits match well with moral leadership skills including compassion, willingness to help others, truthfulness, fairness, and tolerance for divergent thinking (Pernick, 2002).

Another possible area from which to draw academic leaders is from the legal affairs side of the house. Most universities have in-house counsel who are involved in academics on a day-to-day basis over issues such as tenure, promotion, shared governance, catalogues, and policies. Since CAOs must understand legal issues that affect higher education and how state and federal rules influence strategic decision making (Townsend and Bassoppo-Moyo, 1997), a background in law is helpful.

Academy member librarians have traditionally been seen only as remote candidates for roles in academic affairs. Looking into the future (which is already here!), academic officers will need more than a cursory understanding of instructional technology. A background in this area could be excellent preparation for a CAO. Closer study would indicate that library administrators are experienced in these areas, as well as in fiscal and political arenas. They are also frequently skilled in brokering cooperation among campus constituencies. With planned exposure to the broader campus community, many librarians could be cross-trained to serve in CAO roles.

Other equally important issues CAOs must deal with that are outside the realm of the typical academic arena are construction and repair of physical plant, fundraising, management of student housing and auxiliary services, maintenance and operations of the student learning environment, marketing and recruiting, campus security and safety, and staff training and retention (Kennedy, 2001). Whether moving directly from one of these roles or from roles with responsibility for oversight of them, prospective CAOs will benefit from knowledge and experience in all of these areas.

What Strategies to Implement to Foster Diversity in Academic Leadership

Perhaps the most critical aspect in identifying, encouraging, and employing academic officers from outside the academic arena is to create a culture of change within the college or university. First, this is necessary to overcome fears of giving up everything for which a student affairs officer or other administrator has trained and anxiety over losing the personal satisfaction found in their current roles for the criticism, hassle, and extra commitments inherent in academic administration. (This case might also need to be made to convince a faculty member to move from the classroom to the boardroom.) A culture where change is accepted would also increase the likelihood that faculty would accept a CAO from outside traditional career paths.

In addition to the fear of changing roles, potential candidates for CAO positions need to recognize that all executive officer roles are difficult regardless of the area of responsibility. Sacrifices, both personal and professional, must be made for the betterment of the college or university. Also, the feelings of isolation and loneliness that executives often feel may increase the stress normally felt with new job adjustments. To survive the transition, candidates should be prepared to expect long hours, interpersonal conflicts, and accusations of having gone to "the dark side." Often the greatest dilemma is whether the candidate has the stamina for executive leadership rather than personal competency or previous administrative experiences. A self-motivated leader, with support from the president, can successfully make the transition into academic affairs and deal with the complexity and challenges inherent in academic leadership roles.

Leadership Development Activities

As institutions develop succession planning strategies and look to others within the organization to assume a role in academic affairs, leadership development activities must be instituted to broaden internal applicant pools. An institution may put together a variety of in-house or external leadership development programs.

Leadership training programs should identify campus leaders who are competent in their existing roles and are able to realize that their skill sets may be transferable to the world of academia. The positive perspective of implementing this concept to fill open positions outside the traditional academy pool may breathe fresh air into the university.

Leadership training institutes are prevalent and are offered by many professional organizations and colleges that see the wisdom of grooming current administrators in the organization's culture (Anderson, 1997). Professional societies may highlight the formal and informal aspects of educational leadership and fill the skills gap that graduate programs leave (Laden, 1996). In addition, larger institutions may establish their own leadership development activities and can thus exercise greater control of their destinies if they identify their own future executive officers.

Mentoring is also very important as a way of developing and encouraging future leaders from across the college or university. Intergenerational mentoring can help promote a strong transition for newly identified academic leaders (Rao, 1998). Regardless of the mentored activity, aspiring academic leaders would be wise to develop a "portfolio of experiences . . . volunteering for committees or projects where administrative-like activities occur" (Cejda, McKenney, and Burley, 2001, p. 42).

In many respects, the faculty of current graduate schools determine the future leadership of educational institutions (Townsend and Bassoppo-Moyo, 1996). They accept prospective students, develop and implement the curricula for higher education administration, and from this closed setting produce a large number of future leaders (Townsend and Bassoppo-Moyo, 1996). These programs need to recognize the value of diversity in the background of academic officers and support the fresh perspectives they bring to academic leadership.

Diversity must extend beyond disciplines and promote the inclusion of minorities and females. Establishing a leadership conduit for future academic deans and vice presidents is also critical for the future of historically black colleges and universities, and Hargrove (2000) recommends that planning initiatives be put in place to identify and mentor leaders during the first ten years of their career. Despite advances made in recent years, traditional enrollment trends have not changed so dramatically that large pools of African American leaders are emerging from higher education graduate programs.

In the past, an outstanding staff member in administrative or student services may have been prevented from consideration for an executive-level appointment because he or she did not possess the traditional doctorate degree. As more nontraditional graduate programs become available through distance education, this barrier to crossing over into academic administration may be eliminated, at least in community colleges. Universities will likely continue to require the doctorate for the highest level of academic leadership.

Conclusion

Deans and vice presidents today are responsible for personnel, budgets, regulations, and other managerial components similar to those found in private industry. No longer does it follow that because the position is housed in academics, the CAO must be classically trained as a faculty member.

Administrative service officers, financial managers, student affairs officers, and other administrators may lack the classic liberal arts background and teaching experience of many university faculty, but they may bring skills in managing physical assets, prioritizing political and strategic plans, building strong teams, and serving students in a multitude of ways. Depending on the president's background, the skills they bring to the executive team may be exactly what is needed to complement the composition of the management structure.

The chief academic officer in today's institution of higher education does not have to be a subject or discipline expert. His or her role is to respect the tenets of the academy and ensure that academic freedom remains intact. Using the communication skills that are appropriate to that level of executive administration, he or she can bridge the gap with teaching faculty and earn respect as their representative. Although many faculty in higher education disavow this belief, the CAO needs to be more of an academic manager than a discipline expert.

The nature of leadership is changing in many venues, and education is not an exception. The person with the right leadership fit is more likely to be successful than someone who has the traditional formal training in academics. The innovative institution realizes this and encourage others to cross the great divide.

References

Anderson, J. A. "Leadership Training Initiatives for Community College Administrators: A Focused Synthesis of the Literature." *Community College Review,* 1997, *24,* 27–54.
Bragg, D. D. "Preparing Community College Deans to Lead Change." *New Directions for Community Colleges,* 2000, *109,* 75–85.

Cejda, B. D., McKenney, C. B., and Burley, H. "The Career Lines of Chief Academic Officers in Public Community Colleges." *Community College Review,* 2000, 28(4), 31–46.

Hargrove, S. K. "Developing Faculty for Academic Leadership." *Black Issues in Higher Education,* 2000, 19(24), 90.

Kennedy, M. "The Top Ten Issues Impacting College Administrators." *American School and University,* 2001, 73(5), 23–28.

Laden, B. V. "The Role of Professional Associations in Developing Academic and Administrative Leaders." *New Directions for Community Colleges,* 1996, 95, 47–58.

Mech, T. F. "The Managerial Roles of Chief Academic Officers." *Journal of Higher Education,* 1997, 68, 282–298.

Murray, J. P., and Murray, J. I. "The Propensity of Community College Chief Academic Officers to Leave an Institution." *Community College Review,* 2000, 28(3), 22–36.

Pernick, R. "Creating a Leadership Development Program: Nine Essential Tasks." *Public Management,* 2002, 84(7), 10–17.

Rao, M. "Developing New Leaders: The Role of Relationships." *Change,* 1998, 30, 46–48.

Thomas, W. "The Moral Domain of Student Affairs Leadership." *New Directions for Student Services,* 2002, 98, 61–70.

Townsend, B. K., and Bassoppo-Moyo, S. "The Effective Community College Academic Administrator: Necessary Competencies and Attitudes." *Community College Review,* 1997, 25, 41–56.

Twombly, S. B. "Administrative Labor Markets." *Journal of Higher Education,* 1988, 59(6), 668–689.

PATRICIA C. LAND *is Charlotte Campus president of Edison College in Punta Gorda, Florida.*

3

The complex responsibilities of academic leadership require multidimensional training, exemplified in the six principles undergirding the internationally recognized program examined here.

Six Critical Issues for Midlevel Leadership in Postsecondary Settings

Gary L. Filan, Alan T. Seagren

Researchers have spent years investigating the demands, multiple roles, and critical nature of organizational leaders in postsecondary educational settings. Overall, the research indicates agreement that leadership at all levels in postsecondary education is complex and multidimensional. During the past thirty years, though, much of the research has concentrated specifically on the capacious role of midlevel leadership, with the main focus on academic department chairs within colleges and universities. Research validates that leading from the middle is no easy task. Gmelch and Miskin (1993), Seagren and others (1994), and Lucas (2000) document the multipart role of the midlevel management in higher education, and Tucker (1993) lists fifty-five duties that chairs perform.

Research by Diamond (1996), Hecht, Higgerson, Gmelch, and Tucker (1999), and Lucas (2000) finds that the roles and responsibilities of the department chair have been expanded over the decade. Pettitt's research (1999) confirms that "chairs are critical to the college's effectiveness in carrying out its mission and realizing its vision for the future" (p. 64). Lucas (2000) argues that the increasing emphasis on accountability and performance-based management, as well as leading change and high-performance teams, contributes significantly to the multifarious nature of leadership at the department chair level in postsecondary education.

Contact the authors at The Academy for Leadership Training and Development, 145 North Centennial Way, Mesa, AZ 85201 or electronically at www.mc.maricopa.edu/chair for further detail and discussion.

NEW DIRECTIONS FOR HIGHER EDUCATION, no. 124, Winter 2003 © Wiley Periodicals, Inc.

Given the research findings over the past thirty years and the range of issues facing higher education in the first few years of this new century, it appears logical to predict a continuing increase in role demands and complexity. The purpose of this chapter is not to reiterate the roles or to predict specific future roles and responsibilities, but to argue for the integration of what we know and can predict about expansive academic leadership duties at the midlevel in postsecondary organizations. This chapter focuses on these issues and key components of skills and competencies as they relate specifically to transformational leadership. But before we discuss the critical issues, we need to establish the context of our work.

The Evolution of a Leadership Training Model

Historically, leadership training has been designed for postsecondary deans and vice presidents to prepare them for a presidency. Few, if any, opportunities have been available to chairs or midlevel managers even though they outnumber all other types of administrators combined. Unlike the private sector, which devotes a considerable percentage of its training dollars to midlevel managers, higher education provides minimal funds for this level. Thus, although the midlevel manager or chair position is widely regarded as key to the effective functioning of a college or university's major academic programs, those filling the positions generally receive little or no formal training for the job. This is especially the case for academic department chairs. In 1992, the department chairs of the Maricopa Community Colleges, located in the Phoenix metropolitan area of Arizona, recognized this need for training and committed to identifying and supporting the resources needed to obtain the necessary skills to lead their departments effectively.

The grassroots movement, initiated by the Maricopa department chairs, has evolved into the Academy for Leadership Training and Development, an internationally recognized program. The academy began in 1992 with the International Conference for Chairs, Deans, and Other Organizational Leaders and focused on providing leadership development for midlevel managers. In addition to designing the first annual international conference, the department chairs of the Maricopa Community Colleges also began to research and design a more extensive training program for academic and administrative leadership to meet the needs of midlevel organizational leaders. These efforts eventually developed into the Academy for Leadership Training and Development, which now offers leadership training programs throughout the United States, Canada, South Pacific, Australia, Europe, and the Middle East. Statewide programs are offered in Wisconsin, New Jersey, New York, Michigan, Florida, Iowa, and Illinois, as well as provincewide programs in Ontario and Alberta. Local, customized leadership programs are available as well. In addition, national and international programs offer opportunities for global connections among postsecondary leaders. By the end of summer 2003, more than thirty-five hundred leaders had benefited from the academy's program.

The Academy Leadership Program provides a systems approach to transformational leadership, with training occurring over time with measured outcomes. Two weeks of residential training, bridged by a year-long practicum with support mechanisms for coaching and mentoring in the participant's current college position, provide the foundation for the program. Participant leaders are networked with mentors on their own campuses and with colleagues from their leadership class. Ongoing personal and electronic conversations keep leaders connected to each other, their campuses, experienced leaders, and the academy.

The week-long residential experiences are skillfully developed to introduce key leadership theory, research, and best practices. The year-long practicum is a carefully monitored mentoring experience designed to provide the opportunity to implement an individualized professional development plan, reflective practice and journaling, and situated learning. In addition, leaders are subscribed to a listserv that provides up-to-date leadership information, support, and opportunities for discussion. The listserv allows leaders to continue interacting and sharing ideas with one another beyond the residential experiences.

Academy training is facilitated by a cadre of program graduates who continue in leadership positions in higher education. These graduates are chosen for their knowledge and skill in facilitation and for their ongoing commitment to best practices in leadership on their own campuses. They model coaching, stewardship, and lifelong learning through their dedication and continued study of exemplary practices and the current theory and research on leadership. They are committed to developing new leaders.

The goal of the academy is to provide relevant, learner-centered training and professional development that is engaging, meaningful, and useful, resulting in change and professional growth. For those academy participants who are pursuing advanced degree programs, graduate-level credit partnerships have been solidified between the academy and several respected universities, including the University of Nebraska and University of Wisconsin in the United States, University of Toronto in Canada, and Victoria University in Australia. Graduates of the academy can earn up to nine hours of credit toward a master's or doctoral degree.

The academy is not designed as, and was never intended to be, a program for promoting leaders. It was designed to meet the specific knowledge and skills needed for people to be effective transformational leaders at the midlevel. A large numbers of academy graduates have been promoted, but their promotion was a result of their personal goals and initiatives. Many academy graduates have remained in midlevel leadership positions and more effectively serve their colleges, faculty, and students as a result of the program. The program emphasizes that higher education needs transformational leaders at all levels of the organization, not just at the top.

The academy works to convert Covey's goal for training programs into a reality. "Programs should attempt to empower people to soar, to sail, to step forward bravely into the unknown" (Covey, 1992, p. 72). Evidence of success of such empowerment is abundant among academy graduates, largely because the academy practices one of Covey's seven habits of highly successful people: beginning with the end in mind (Covey, 1990). Pam Bergeron, director of employee relations at Lansing Community College in Lansing, Michigan, and an academy graduate, wrote, "My life changed in a hundred different ways that week. I feel reenergized, confident, experienced, and wise. The academy has been a metamorphosis for me. I only hope that I can share this experience and the direction and expertise I've gained from it with those leaders, and potential leaders, who dare to embark on this wonderful journey."

Critical Components of Leadership

Six critical issues associated with leadership in higher education serve as the basis for academy training:

- Understanding self
- Understanding transformational leadership
- Establishing and maintaining relationships
- Leading teams
- Leading strategic planning and change
- Connecting through community

The academy offers opportunities to understand major research and theoretical developments in leadership for each of these six critical components. Participants have opportunities to develop proficiency in selecting, integrating, and applying appropriate concepts from social and behavioral science and adult education in formulating and implementing approaches to leadership problems and issues.

As we discuss each of these critical issues, we will also briefly describe the Academy Leadership Program to illustrate the competencies developed during the course of the year-long program. We highlight key learning opportunities and provide testimony from leaders in postsecondary education who have successfully completed the year-long program.

Understanding Self. While scholars have been examining the effect of self-understanding on leadership for centuries, today a focus on the moral and ethical dimensions of leadership pervades the popular leadership press. Covey (1992) is perhaps foremost in indicating leadership needs to be principle centered, pointing out that individuals are more effective and organizations are more empowered when they are guided and governed by proven principles. These principles surface in the form of values, ideas, norms, and teachings that uplift, ennoble, fulfill, empower, and inspire people (Covey,

1992). Beginning with a personal mission statement, Covey (1990) offers the foundation on which to build a framework to manage the complex roles and responsibilities of leadership. A personal mission statement articulates the most basic self-understanding of what we value, what we want to accomplish, a code of conduct, ethics, and communication.

The Leadership Academy provides in-depth investigations into knowledge and understanding of self. Academy participants begin by assessing the expectations and demands of their colleagues, colleges, and students. Participants reflect on responsibility to balance job, family, lifestyle, and well-being. Personal values are integrated holistically. The personal mission statement becomes the foundation for professional mission statements.

Throughout the training and development at the academy, participants continue to explore the understanding of self by moving from personal and professional mission statements, through the changing roles of organizational leaders, understanding communication principles, and learning the value of being a servant leader in today's postsecondary organizations. They have the opportunity to investigate, experience, and reflect on their personal style and behaviors as leaders. Kragness and Rening (1996) points out that leadership is based in behavior and not in authority or position. Kouzes and Posner (2002) suggest that effective leaders do not control others but rather create an environment that enables others to be successful. Effective leaders create this environment by understanding themselves and others.

Surveys and instruments assist in the process of self-understanding and learning how to adjust communication and work-style behaviors to meet the needs of others. During the course of the year-long program, the academy uses several tools: self-report, supervisor evaluation, peer evaluator, and questionnaires. Using these tools for insights into personal tendencies and behaviors is a helpful step toward self-understanding. When leaders look at themselves during the academy experience with the assistance of behavioral style, personality style, communication style, leadership style, or learning style instruments, they become increasingly aware of their attitudes and behaviors. These instruments also enhance appreciation and understanding of style differences in others, providing the foundation for increased willingness to be open to discoveries about one's self, as well as ways to work more effectively with others.

When discussing the power of the Personal Profile System, one participant, Grace Williams, assistant director for human resources at Kalamazoo Valley Community College, in Kalamazoo, Michigan, wrote, "I had taken this instrument prior to coming to the academy. Revisiting and comparing my results from before, I now understand that the benefit of this instrument is not only in focusing on the strengths and limitations of my own style, but also in identifying the work styles of people I interact with on a daily basis. Taking this instrument alone as a single event limited my understanding, however, but when the instrument and the learning derived from it were integrated into all topics in the program, I learned specific skills to help me as a leader to try to adjust to meet the style needs of those with whom I work." Instruments that promote such self-understanding affirm Bennis's argument (1997) that leadership is a function of knowing yourself.

Understanding Transformational Leadership. The second key issue that integrates the roles and responsibilities of today's leaders is transformational leadership. Transformational leaders, according to Burns (1978), engage the full person so that followers are developed into leaders. They raise followers' level of awareness of the importance of achieving valued outcomes and of strategies for reaching them. Transformational leaders support followers' needs to move to higher levels of achievement while simultaneously encouraging them to transcend their own self-interests for the sake of the team, organization, or larger policy.

Burns (1978) avows that understanding the distinction between transformational and transactional leadership is essential in higher education. Generally, the transactional leader works within the organizational culture as it exists; the transformational leader works at changing the organizational culture. The transactional leader pursues a cost-benefit or an economic exchange to meet subordinates' current material and psychic needs in return for contracted services rendered by the subordinate. The transformational leader also recognizes these existing needs in potential followers but tends to go further, seeking to arouse and satisfy higher needs and engage the full person.

When academic leaders practice transformational leadership, they become a source of inspiration to faculty, staff, administrators, and students. Transformational leaders model the work of Bass and Avolio (1990) when they diagnose, meet, and elevate the needs of all members of the organization through individualized consideration, stimulate followers to view the world of postsecondary education from new perspectives, and inspire trust in the leader to affect organizational growth and change positively.

Establishing and Maintaining Relationships. The third key issue that integrates the roles and responsibilities of today's leaders is establishing and maintaining relationships. In discussing this issue, Wheatley (1999) points out that leaders must engage the whole system, create openness, circulate abundant information, and develop simple reporting systems in their efforts to establish and maintain effective communication. She argued that relationship development must be a leader's top priority. She also reminded us that trust is the leader's greatest asset and that leaders should resist competitive behaviors, supporting only collaboration in dealing effectively with issues and responsibilities. Appreciating a kaleidoscope of views, behaviors, work, and learning styles is central to communication in postsecondary organizations today. Drawing on the collective expertise of all within the organization while maintaining a concern for the personal identity of each individual on the team is an essential quality of leaders. Creativity and trust are hallmarks of environments in which people feel respected, valued, and appreciated.

Recent work by Kouzes and Posner (2002) and McKenna and Maister (2002) offers additional insights into understanding relationship development as the key to successful leadership. McKenna and Maister (2002) reported, "Your technical competence and knowledge will determine a small portion of your effectiveness as a group leader. The overwhelming determinant of whether or not you will be effective has to do with your people skills—interpersonal, social, and emotional" (p. 27). Kouzes and Posner (2002) list three essential relationship skills for leadership success: "Listen deeply to others, discover and appeal to a common purpose, and give life to a vision by communicating expressively, so that people can see themselves in it" (p. 148).

Today's leaders must be skilled communicators able to read nonverbal messages, encode encouraging and motivating messages, influence others through behavior and language, give and receive feedback, provide honest and encouraging appraisals, value individuals while coaching for improved performance, communicate clearly with a wide variety of audiences, communicate optimism, and motivate and inspire through words. Understanding and developing knowledge and skill in establishing and maintaining relationships through communication is critical in meeting the multiple and overlapping responsibilities of postsecondary leadership.

Leading Teams. Leading teams is the fourth key issue deployed in the academy's training programs. Research by Katzenbach and Smith (1992), Matusak (1997), Kees (1997), Blanchard (2000), MacMillan (2001), and Maxwell (2001) substantiates the intricate obligations of leaders in building and leading high-performance teams. Judith Limkilde, dean of applied arts and health sciences at Seneca College in King City, Ontario, and an academy graduate, confirms her understanding of leadership teams: "Learning how to build, monitor, coach, and evaluate the progress of teams has been a real asset in my position. To be able to pinpoint task and process roles, to understand the processes of consensus seeking, to strive for better work style balance on teams, to recognize team functions and potential dysfunctions—these have all been critical to my success as a leader."

Matusak (1997) spent two years assessing components of educational leadership for the Kellogg Foundation. Her findings suggest that the most compelling issues for today's higher education leaders are visioning, initiating, guiding, and encouraging with and through teams. O'Banion (1997) points out that if institutions are to become more learning centered, leaders, especially at the department chair level, need to be "other focused" and model teamwork.

Insights into high-performance teams (Katzenbach and Smith, 1992), coupled with the skills-based approach offered by Kees (2001), facilitate development in building and leading teams. Leaders must understand the stages of team development, process, and task roles of team members; work through differences and achieve consensus; and manage conflict productively (Kees, 2001). As team leaders, postsecondary leaders must learn the important communication skills of directing, teaching, coaching, consulting, and facilitating to meet the needs of individuals and teams as they work to achieve significant organizational outcomes. Lucas (2000) points out that "members of a team need to develop expertise in creating a climate of trust and support, using active listening, managing conflict creatively, problem solving and decision making, and cultivating interpersonal effectiveness in small groups" (p. 15). Recognizing how to build, monitor, and coach teams is thus critical for today's college and university leaders. Jim Plog, director of staff and organizational development at Northeast Wisconsin Technical College in Green Bay, Wisconsin, and an academy graduate, confirms his development as a team leader: "Learning to coach individuals and teams through tough challenges was perhaps the single most important skill I learned in the academy. Leading teams is central to my role. The academy taught me how to use and lead teams effectively."

In her synthesis of physical science principles and social change, Wheatley (1992) reminds us that people support what they create and recreate. As leaders build and lead teams, they facilitate staff and organizations where collaboration is the hallmark of success. Collaboration requires learning to work on teams, handling conflict, making decisions through consensus, demonstrating ethical process, and using team assessment.

Leading Strategic Planning and Change. Critical thinking, scenario planning, and managing change are essential tasks of academic leaders. Critical thinking requires analytical and problem-solving skills to build a solid understanding of the present in planning for the future. Scenario planning can then be a very powerful tool that assists staff in thinking about options and preparing them for dealing with the changing environment of higher education. This process is facilitated by involving team members from design to implementation. Bryson (1989) indicates that it is strategic thinking and acting that are important, not just strategic planning. The plan itself, the product of the planning process, is secondary in importance to the change in the quality of thinking and acting that result from the process. Effective planning creates focus, direction, and energy. Most important, strategic plans can assist in building a shared commitment to a common future.

Strategic planning provides direction, identifies purpose and mission, and drives the use and allocation of fiscal resources. It provides the framework to deal with external and internal forces faced by departments and colleges in today's rapidly changing environments. It should lead to change within individuals and within the organization.

Connecting Through Community. The final integrated key issue for leadership is connecting individuals, teams, departments, and the college itself with the community. Clearly, leaders must bridge their teams to the larger organizational culture. However, the linkages do not stop at the borders of the campus. Connecting through community requires leadership that goes beyond the boundaries of the campus into the environment in which the college functions. Academic leaders must build communities of practice on their campuses and encourage, support, and lead connections from campus constituencies to other educational levels, business and industry, professional associations, and the community at large.

As leaders connect individuals, teams, and communities, they are increasingly reminded that simply bringing individuals and communities together is not enough. The intricate linkages require encouragement, inspiration, empowerment, and then recognition and celebration of contributions. Kouzes and Posner (2002) encourage leaders to build community by celebrating values and victories together. Celebrating community reinforces the fact that extraordinary performance is the result of many people's efforts: "By celebrating people's accomplishments visibly and in group settings, leaders create and sustain team spirit; by basing celebrations on the accomplishment of key values and milestones, they sustain people's focus" (p. 368).

The academy builds a learning community among the participants, sustains the community through high-performance leadership challenges, and recognizes the accomplishments of each individual as he or she completes the rigorous year-long program. Most important, the academy builds, sustains, and celebrates a community of higher education leaders who have become exemplars of transformational leadership worldwide.

Conclusion

Integrating the roles and responsibilities of postsecondary leaders within the six critical issues discussed in this chapter provides a framework for understanding the knowledge and skill competencies necessary for midlevel higher education into the next decade.

The Academy for Leadership Training and Development is an example of professional development that offers leaders the knowledge and skill competencies to meet the challenges of leadership in today's postsecondary settings. Elsie Elford, dean of the College of Business at Grant MacEwan College in Edmonton, Alberta, writes, "I attended the academy in 1993. I was a new chair having just joined postsecondary education from the private sector. I was not confident about my abilities or my role as a department chair. The academy facilitated my personal growth and confidence. I can't tell you how much I learned and grew over the year-long academy. Since the academy, I have continued to be involved in academy programs and conferences. The academy has continued to support me in my growth and confidence as an academic leader." This testimonial and others in this chapter, along with the hundreds of others garnered over the years from academy participants, are clear evidence that midlevel administrators benefit from a transformational leadership program.

References

Bass, B. M., and Avolio, B. J. *Manual for the Multifactor Leadership Questionnaire.* Palo Alto, Calif.: Consulting Psychologists Press, 1990.

Bennis, W. *Managing People Is Like Herding Cats.* Provo, Utah: Executive Excellence Publishing, 1997.

Blanchard, K. H. *The One Minute Manager Builds High Performing Teams.* New York: Quill, 2000.

Bryson, J. M. *Strategic Planning for Public and Nonprofit Organizations: A Guide to Strengthening and Sustaining Organizational Achievement.* San Francisco: Jossey-Bass, 1989.

Burns, J. M. *Leadership.* New York: HarperCollins, 1978.

Covey, S. R. *The Seven Habits of Highly Effective People.* New York: Fireside Press, 1990.

Covey, S. R. *Principle-Centered Leadership.* New York: Simon & Schuster, 1992.

Diamond, R. M. "What It Takes to Lead a Department." *Chronicle of Higher Education,* Jan. 5, 1996, 42(17), pp. B1–B2.

Gmelch, W. H., and Miskin, B. D. *Leadership Skills for Department Chairs.* Bolton, Mass.: Anker, 1993.

Hecht, I. W., Higgerson, M. L., Gmelch, W. H., and Tucker, A. *The Department Chair as Academic Leader.* Phoenix, Ariz.: American Council on Education and Oryx Press, 1999.

Katzenbach, J., and Smith, D. *The Wisdom of Teams: Creating the High-Performance Organization.* Boston: Harvard Business School Press, 1992.

Kees, F. *Teamwork from Start to Finish.* San Francisco: Pfeiffer, 1997.

Kees, F. *How to Lead Work Teams.* San Francisco: Jossey-Bass, 2001.

Kouzes, J. M., and Posner, B. Z. *The Leadership Challenge.* (3rd ed.) San Francisco: Jossey-Bass, 2002.

Kragness, M. E., and Rening, L. *A Comparison of the Personal Profile System and the Myers-Briggs Type Indicator.* Minneapolis: Carlson Learning Company, 1996.

Lucas, A. F. *Leading Academic Change: Essential Roles for Department Chairs.* San Francisco: Jossey-Bass, 2000.

MacMillan, P. *The Performance Factor: Unlocking the Secrets of Teamwork.* New York: Broadman and Holman, 2001.

Matusak, L. R. *Finding Your Voice: Learning to Lead. . . . Anywhere You Want to Make a Difference.* San Francisco: Jossey-Bass, 1997.

Maxwell, J. C. *The Seventeen Indisputable Laws of Teamwork.* Nashville, Tenn.: Thomas Nelson, 2001.

McKenna, P. J., and Maister, D. H. *First Among Equals.* New York: Free Press, 2002.

O'Banion, T. S. *A Learning College for the Twenty-First Century.* Phoenix, Ariz.: Oryx Press, 1997.

Pettitt, J. M. *Situating Midlevel Managers' Training: Learning and Doing in Context. Preparing Department Chairs for Their Leadership Roles.* New Directions for Community Colleges, no. 105. San Francisco: Jossey-Bass, 1999.

Seagren, A. T., and others. *Academic Leadership in Community Colleges.* Lincoln: University of Nebraska Press, 1994.

Tucker, A. *Chairing the Academic Department: Leadership Among Peers.* Phoenix: Oryx Press, 1993.

Wheatley, M. J. *Leadership and the New Science: Learning About Organizations from an Orderly Universe.* San Francisco: Berrett-Koehler, 1992.

Wheatley, M. J. *Leader to Leader.* San Francisco: Drucker Foundation and Jossey-Bass, 1999.

GARY L. FILAN is one of the founders and executive director of the Chair Academy, a program of the Maricopa Community Colleges, Phoenix, Arizona.

ALAN T. SEAGREN is a professor and director of the Center for Postsecondary and Higher Education at the University of Nebraska, Lincoln, Nebraska.

4

While the best professional development for aspiring administrators may simply be to spend time in the company of leaders, more formal experiences can entail internship, mentor alignment, and institutes.

The Role of Professional Development in Preparing Academic Leaders

Shirley C. Raines, Martha Squires Alberg

"Important? Definitely. Overworked? Probably. Prepared for the job? Rarely. This is the typical academic department chairperson" (Bennett, 1983, p. 1). Although these words were written more than two decades ago, most faculty who have made their first foray into the world of administration would agree that Bennett's words are as true today as they were then. Just two years ago, Milton Greenberg (2001) wrote, "I too suffered the initial trauma of a chairmanship. Administration is not what most of us are trained to do, or even something most of us aspire to, but it is a necessary part of life anywhere" (p. 1).

Although all academic leaders do not begin their administrative careers as department chairs, for faculty this is a common first step. And it is reasonable to assume that strong department chairs are likely to become college deans, provosts, and presidents. In this chapter, we examine the experiences of academicians-turned-administrators, the role of professional development in facilitating this transition, and the kinds of training and support viewed as most valuable by successful educational leaders.

The Transition from Academia to Administration

An informal poll of colleagues in administration included two university presidents, one community college president, one provost, and two deans of education in four states. One president stated, "Like most leaders in higher education, I did not set out to be a chairman, dean, vice president, or president. Also, I did not participate in any formal training or professional development programs in preparation for any of these positions."

If we believe the old adage that we pay attention to what is important to us, it would appear that higher education in general places low value on administrative roles, particularly the role of chair. A survey of the literature on academic leadership underscores the importance of the chair's position. Bennett (1983) writes, "Whether appointed or elected to the job, the chairperson plays a key role in its workings. It is at the department level that the real institutional business gets conducted—it is here that teachers and learners make contact, that researchers find encouragement and direction, and that many of the ways to contribute to the larger community are identified and explored" (p. 1). Without adequate preparation, however, collegiate leaders rarely have time to develop a philosophy of their role and goals as chairmen; in fact, some may enter their appointments with what Bogue (1994) calls a "flawed vision of role" (p. 9). Bogue's description of these flawed visionaries may be somewhat tongue-in-cheek; however, anyone who has spent time in academia has encountered "leaders" with some of these characteristics:

> There are academic cheerleaders, looking for the parade so that they can get in front. There are status fondlers worrying only about the appearance of their calling card. There are information wizards inundated with computer reports and electronic mail addresses. There are educational firemen occupied with crises of their own making. There are trivia worshipers checking forms in stock and occupying their time and energy with the minutia of their unit or campus, enamored of technique but devoid of vision. There are academic mannequins veneered in status but empty of passion and caring. And there are leadership amateurs attempting to guide a precious enterprise with fluffy and empty notions about the content of their work [p. 9].

Even highly competent and qualified faculty who appear well suited for leadership—the so-called unflawed— "may find the transition difficult in today's large, complex colleges and universities where faculty and administrators fill increasingly different roles and encounter different aspects of the environment. Birnbaum (1988) asserts that administrators "come to be seen by the faculty as ever more remote from the central academic concerns that define the institution." Moreover, as the gap widens, faculty may be viewed by administrators as "self-interested, unconcerned with controlling costs, or unwilling to respond to legitimate requests for accountability" (p. 7). Instead of creating and enjoying a climate in which teaching and scholarship can thrive, new leaders often find themselves feeling misunderstood, unappreciated, inadequate, frustrated, and discouraged.

According to Bennett (1983), a new chairperson must adjust to at least three "major and rather abrupt transitions": a radical shift from specialist to generalist, a shift from being an individualist to running a collective, and a transition from loyalty to one's discipline to loyalty to the institution. As a newly appointed leader recently wrote, "When you apply for a faculty job, it's all about you. When you apply for an administrative job, it's all about what you can do for others" (Bugeja, 2001, p. C4).

Successful chairs who go on to become deans may find themselves less prepared than expected by their departmental leadership experiences. Whereas chairs interact primarily with academics, deans must successfully work with a range of interests, individuals, and groups (Rosser, Johnsrud, and Heck, 2003). The former image of the dean as scholarly leader has been replaced by an executive image of the dean as politically astute and economically savvy (Gmelch, Wolverton, Wolverton, and Sarros, 1999).

Each successive level of academic leadership carries with it new challenges. Each role is shaped not only by the individual holding the position but also by the culture of the college or university. Effective leadership involves planning and adaptation; it also involves interpreting and communicating institutional values and understanding organizational processes (Chaffee and Tierney, 1988).

Preparing for Academic Leadership

There is an extensive general literature on organizational leadership (examples are Bass, 1990; Bolman and Deal, 1984; and McCauley, Moxley, and Van Velsor, 1998). There are also volumes and articles specific to leadership in collegiate settings (among them are Birnbaum, 1992; Bensimon and Neumann, 1993; and Tierney, 1988). A working knowledge of leadership theory is an invaluable resource to a new leader, but all leadership is context specific. We must determine for ourselves how best to apply the theories within the unique culture of our environments.

The best preparation of faculty for academic leadership may be attained by simply being in the company of leaders. Identify individuals in administrative roles who are worthy of emulation, and spend time with them. Talk to them about the nature of their daily work. Serve on committees that will allow you to see them in action. Ask yourself, "Is this the kind of work I want to do?" Each of the successful leaders, when asked informally what development activities had been the most helpful, mentioned at least one admired leader who had served as an example. This presidential comment was typical: "My development came largely through watching and learning from some very good examples and from taking on new tasks whenever I had the opportunity."

The decision that you want to become a department chair, a dean, or a president, that the work of administration is interesting and fulfilling for you, is best made after experience in the role. Consider the chronicle of the year-long search of Joshua R. Foyle (a pseudonym) for a senior administrative position. After several disappointing interviews, he was asked to serve as interim dean of the college. He writes, "Happily, it has only reinforced my desire to serve in a senior administrative role on a permanent basis. Don't get me wrong, each day has not been blissful. There have been challenges every day and some gut-wrenching decisions. But in the final analysis, the semester has been one of the most rewarding for me professionally since I returned to academe 14 years ago" (Foyle, 2001, p. C3).

A formal administrative internship can offer not only hands-on experience and a comprehensive view of the administrator's world but also a gateway to administrative positions. Internships associated with degree programs in leadership or administration provide the ideal training ground for prospective leaders. Although faculty are unlikely to have the luxury of full-time, formal internship opportunities, several successful leaders interviewed for this chapter reported informal internship experiences that helped them decide to pursue permanent positions and redirect their careers toward academic administration. They might have filled in for a chair who was on sabbatical, absent for health reasons, or making the transition to retirement. Perhaps they served in an interim leadership role. In either case, they were able to experience firsthand the kinds of activities and decisions that are components of academic leadership and determine for themselves if this work suited them.

If filling a leadership position temporarily to gain administrative experience is not feasible, serving on policymaking or other administrative committees can provide a sense of the day-to-day work associated with administration in academia. The decisions made by committee may not be necessarily either blissful or gut wrenching, but participation in the process provides a closer look at both the peaks and valleys of this kind of leadership role.

In addition to actually doing administrative work, new leaders may be formally or informally linked with an experienced administrator who serves as a mentor. Mentorship is often discussed as beneficial to the personal and professional development of individuals new to their field. This is particularly true in P–12 education, where policymakers have emphasized the inclusion of mentoring programs in efforts to improve the instructional performance of schools (Carnegie Task Force on Teaching as a Profession, 1986; Furtwengler, 1995).

Faculty members moving into administration are not generally wet-behind-the-ears youngsters eager to be molded by a veteran. Rather, they are experienced academicians who need to learn new processes in a very short time period so that they can function effectively. Sometimes an experienced colleague whose leadership you admire can provide advice and counsel as you encounter unexpected hurdles in a new role, but the traditional P–12 mentoring model, one that pairs a single mentor with one or more protégés for planned interaction over time, is not currently viewed as a viable option for higher education.

Mentoring is changing in business too, and new approaches being used in the corporate world make sense for academia. In 1997, Intel, a well-known name in business and home computing, formally reinvented its old approach to mentoring to "teach, inspire, and reconnect its employees" (Warner, 2002, p. 116). Warner describes mentoring in this article as "an old fashioned idea [that] can be updated to work perfectly—even in an industry that changes with stunning speed." She continues, "Traditional mentoring tethered an up-and-comer to an old hand for years of personal development and career advice. It was an approach that seemed best-suited for slow-moving industries operating in more stable times" (p. 116). Now, Intel helps link new leaders with multiple "experts" across the organization based on their knowledge needs. These connections are not expected to be long-term mentoring relationships in the traditional sense but are short-term, focused, planned professional development opportunities.

Even today, academic administration is rarely described as changing with stunning speed, but like every other aspect of our lives today, it rarely operates at a leisurely pace. Connecting with individuals who have knowledge you need, regardless of their position in the organization, is just a commonsense idea that Intel has formalized. In the academic environment, the mentoring message to new administrators is to seek assistance from individuals across the campus, reaching across typical academic silos to form mutually beneficial networks for knowledge sharing. Use the expertise outside your college or department by identifying individuals in such areas as business, finance, personnel, and affirmative action to serve as "mentors" in administrative knowledge and skills areas necessary for departmental, college, or institutional leadership.

New leaders who seek mentoring relationships outside their own departments or colleges are likely to benefit in many ways. In fact, a study of collegiate leadership conducted by Bensimon and Neumann (1993) concluded, "Administrators and other leaders who persist in conventional leadership practices, for example, focusing on the thinking and agenda of just one person or just one type of person, are likely to become less and less effectual as the worlds and realities around them change" (p. 135). Today's complex world has produced emerging new interdisciplinary fields of study such as bioinformatics and biotechnologies. Colleges and universities across the country must become more interdisciplinary in nature or risk being hopelessly outdated.

Every administrator polled for this chapter mentioned the value of institutes and seminars provided by national associations as professional development opportunities. The American Association of Colleges for Teacher Education, for example, sponsors the annual New Deans' Institute. The annual meeting of the American Society for Engineering Education features the New Deans' Forum, and the Council of Graduate Schools holds the New Deans' Institute and Summer Workshop. For college and university presidents, the Harvard School of Education hosts the New Presidents' Seminar. There are several nationally recognized leadership development programs for community college leaders, including the Chair Academy affiliated with Maricopa Community Colleges and the John Rousche leadership development programs at the University of Texas. These are outstanding opportunities to obtain discipline-specific as well as general knowledge and to interact and network with peers.

Growing in the Leadership Role

The successful leader in academic administration must find time and opportunity to obtain feedback and engage in continuous self-improvement based on that feedback. Bensimon and Neumann (1993) say, "It is important for administrators and other leaders to acquire a multidimensional view of what they are doing, intentionally or not, to others outside their leadership circle. . . . It is especially important for administrators who are intent on discerning the reality of change in the classrooms, dorms, and campus grounds, and also on responding to change with sensitivity and meaning" (p. 135).

One way of guiding professional growth through reflective practice is the benchmarking or 360-degree feedback process developed by the Center for Creative Leadership in Greensboro, North Carolina, and commonly used in corporate environments to assist managers in improving their performance (McCauley, Moxley, and Van Velsor, 1998). Parallel instrumentation for self-assessment and evaluation by major referent groups (supervisors, peers, and direct reports) provide multidimensional data to assist leaders in developing professional growth plans and achieving optimum performance. Whether through a formal process such as this or a more informal data-gathering structure, a reflective leader can benefit greatly from knowledge about the expectations and perceptions of colleagues regarding their performance in the multiple and complex roles associated with leadership.

When asked what advice he would give to a faculty member moving into an administrative leadership role to help prepare for success, a relatively new and already successful dean replied, "Listen. Listen some more. Think about what you hear. Maintain a broad perspective, and learn to speak clearly and directly about your own perspective." This is the approach that supports reflective practice.

Conclusion

Recent studies conclude that the definition of leadership is local and affected by context and that it is socially constructed among people (Bolman and Deal, 1984; Tierney, 1988). We can learn about budgets, diversity and equity, personnel management, and a host of other topics through professional development, but as Bolman and Deal (1984) so eloquently conclude, "The heart of leadership lies in the hearts of leaders" (p. 6). The good higher education administrator is one who masters the knowledge and skills to perform necessary tasks with efficiency and effectiveness; the outstanding leader engages in reflective practice and continuous growth.

References

Bass, B. *Bass and Stodgill's Handbook of Leadership.* New York: Free Press, 1990.

Bennett, J. B. *Managing the Academic Department.* New York: Macmillan, 1983.

Bensimon, E. M., and Neumann, A. *Redesigning Collegiate Leadership.* Baltimore: Johns Hopkins University Press, 1993.

Birnbaum, R. *How Colleges Work: The Cybernetics of Academic Organizations and Leadership.* San Francisco: Jossey-Bass, 1988.

Birnbaum, R. *How Academic Leadership Works.* San Francisco: Jossey-Bass, 1992.

Bogue, E. G. *Leadership by Design.* San Francisco: Jossey-Bass, 1994.

Bolman, L., and Deal, T. *Modern Approaches to Understanding and Managing Organizations.* San Francisco: Jossey-Bass, 1984.

Bugeja, M. "From Professor to Administrator." *Chronicle of Higher Education,* June 20, 2001, p. C4.

Carnegie Task Force on Teaching as a Profession. *A Nation Prepared: Teachers for the Twenty-First Century.* New York: Carnegie Corporation, 1986.

Chaffee, E. E., and Tierney, W. G. *Collegiate Culture and Leadership Strategies.* New York: American Council on Education and Macmillan, 1988.

Foyle, J. R. "Opportunity Finally Knocks." *Chronicle of Higher Education,* July 11, 2001, p. C3.

Furtwengler, C. "Beginning Teachers Programs: Analysis of State Actions During the Reform Era." *Education Policy Analysis Archives,* 1995, 3(3), 1–20.

Gmelch, W. H., Wolverton, M., Wolverton, M. I., and Sarros, J. C. "The Academic Dean: An Imperiled Species Searching for Balance." *Research in Higher Education,* 1999, 40, 717–740.

Greenberg, M. "The Not Necessarily Thankless Job of Department Chair." *Chronicle of Higher Education,* June 29, 2001. [http://chroncile.com/jobs/2001/06/2001062901c.htm].

McCauley, C. D., Moxley, R. S., and Van Velsor, E. *The Center for Creative Leadership Handbook of Leadership Development.* San Francisco: Jossey-Bass, 1998.

Rosser, V. J., Johnsrud, L. K., and Heck, R. H. "Academic Deans and Directors: Assessing Their Effectiveness from Individual and Institutional Perspectives." *Journal of Higher Education,* 2003, 74(1), 1–25.

Tierney, W. "Organizational Culture in Higher Education." *Journal of Higher Education,* 1988, 59, 2–21.

Warner, F. "Inside Intel's Mentoring Movement." *Fast Company,* 2002. [http://www.fastcompany.com/magazine/57/chalktalk.html].

SHIRLEY C. RAINES is the president of the University of Memphis in Memphis, Tennessee.

MARTHA SQUIRES ALBERG is assistant dean for P–12 programs in the College of Education at the University of Memphis in Memphis, Tennessee.

5

The transition from faculty to administration roles, as well as full-orbed faculty positions, would be smoother if doctoral programs were expanded to include a focus on collegiality and service.

The Role of Doctoral Programs in Preparing Faculty for Multiple Roles in the Academy

Bruce W. Speck

A persistent and pressing problem in higher education is the "us versus them" mentality between faculty and administrators. Thus, when a faculty member takes an administrative position, the transition from faculty member to administrator is often labeled "going over to the dark side," and the nervous laughter that ensues after the administrative label is affixed to the newly appointed administrator reinforces the uneasiness that faculty friends feel toward their former colleague.

Although the tension between faculty and administrators can have a healthy dimension (promoting the advice and consent of shared governance), by and large the tension is unproductive because it is based on misunderstandings about what the mission of higher education is and what roles faculty and administrators play in fulfilling that mission. Much of the animus could be greatly diminished if faculty were given the opportunity to learn about higher education administration before they become faculty members. Indeed, insights into higher education administration could help prepare future faculty members to be not only more effective faculty members but also more effective administrators. I assert that faculty members qua faculty members are often engaged in various administrative duties and should be prepared to perform those duties. Faculty members qua administrators extend that engagement to full-time work, and therefore formal preparation for administrative duties can have a double function of preparing academics to be effective as academics and as administrators. I propose that doctoral programs, which are the font of aspirants to tenure-track appointments, include in their curricula a healthy dose of study about the full role of the professoriat, including administrative responsibilities. As Green (1988a) notes, "Colleges and universities by their own proclamation are in the business of developing leaders for society. . . . Ironically, the academy has paid little systematic attention to developing its own leaders" (p. 1).

In what follows, I offer suggestions about how doctoral programs might provide a full-orbed view of professorial life, including administrative work, not only to prepare those who hope to become professors to perform well in all that they are required to do as professors but also to provide them insight into university life as a whole. For some, this may extend into formal academic leadership positions. My position at the outset is that doctoral programs in general fail to prepare their students adequately for full-orbed professorial life, and in making suggestions about how to remedy this failure, I address the professorial roles of teaching, service, and collegiality as they intersect with administrative work. I will not discuss the role of scholarship as it intersects with administrative work because the sole focus of most doctoral programs (outside colleges and schools of education) is on the scholarship of a particular discipline. Scholarship is already given an inordinate place in doctoral programs. I discuss what I perceive to be the areas of professorial life that currently are not addressed or not addressed adequately in doctoral programs.

The Fallacy of Adequate Preparation

That those who are trained for the professoriat are given but one part of the training necessary to be successful academics has been recognized nationally, and the increasing number of teaching and learning centers instituted by campuses—as a remedial measure—is one piece of evidence that points to a fundamental flaw in the limited way doctoral students have been prepared for the professoriat. Without a doubt, the one part—the scholarship of a particular discipline, and increasingly a specialization within the discipline—has been seen as the essence of graduate school education. The assumption has been that when a person knows a subject thoroughly, that person will be able to provide others with his or her wealth of information and insights into the subject. This assumption is bankrupt; teaching a subject is not coessential with learning a subject. As Huber (1992) notes, "Teachers are apparently supposed to know how to teach because they have been watching teachers do it since first grade—kind of like learning how to play tennis by sitting in the grandstand" (p. 124). Yet for decades, graduate education in the United States has operated on the assumption that people who will stand before hundreds of classes (and surely, over a long teaching career, thousands of students) need no other engagement in teaching than to become adept scholars. The irony of such an assumption, considering the preeminence of research as the basis for knowledge in doctoral granting institutions in the United States, is almost too delicious to bear.

In effect, the unitary focus on scholarship has left many scholars in the beginning years of their tenure-track appointments with all kinds of questions about what academic life is really about. Thus, when the novice tenure-track appointee asks, "What is required of me?" he or she is not merely asking, "What is required of me at this institution?" but also, "What is required of me as a professor?" Specific answers to that question vary according to the mission of the institution, but is it inappropriate to suggest that a professor's various responsibilities can be logically articulated so that what it is to be a professor can be explained during graduate education?

What Professors Do

In what follows, I outline what professors do, including various administrative functions, in an effort to provide direction for graduate educators who prepare students to become effective higher education professionals.

Professors Teach. The assertion that professors teach will receive faint if any challenge, although the quality and quantity of that teaching certainly has come under attack. However, the assertion that thorough preparation of effective teachers for higher education has remarkable similarities to the day-to-day administrative work in which department chairs, deans, provosts, and presidents engage may raise eyebrows, particularly because the "us versus them" mentality is based on a fundamental dichotomy between classroom and administrative work. But as Fish (2003) notes, "Administration is, at its heart, an intellectual task" (p. B20). I would add that that intellectual task bears remarkable similarities to the intellectual task of teaching. The skill needed to prepare an effective syllabus (Grunert, 1997), solid assignments (including the professional assessment of those assignments; Bean and Peterson, 1998; Hobson, 1998; Quigley, 1998; Smith, 1998), lectures (deWinstanley and Bjork, 2002; Saroyan, 2000; Vesilind, 2000), and collaborative work among students mirrors the work administrators do when they prepare various written documents, seek effective assessments based on the feedback loop increasingly required by accrediting agencies, address their faculty on various occasions, and appoint, charge, and steer innumerable committees. The skills necessary for effective teaching are not foreign to the skills necessary for effective administration, and wise administrators of graduate programs would do well to provide training that explores and confirms the role that planning, enacting, and evaluating play in both teaching and administration. Corrigan (2002), president of San Francisco State University, says, "Academic administration for me is simply the extension of my role as educator, and both are extensions of my role as citizen" (p. 9). Effective academic administration is simply an extension of the full-bodied professorial role, which includes effective teaching.

Unfortunately, academicians have a fair amount of disdain for the formal study of pedagogy, believing, it appears, that teaching is an individualized art that defies description and cannot be reduced to anything that approximates training in pedagogy. This antipathy to the formal study of pedagogy is aided and abetted by professors' high self-assessments of their teaching. For example, Cross (1977), in a provocative piece of research, demonstrated that professors think they teach quite well, but their self-reported assessments created a mathematical conundrum: "An amazing 94 percent rate themselves as above-average teachers, and 68 percent rank themselves in the top quarter on teaching performance" (p. 10). This mathematical impossibility is particularly startling when we realize that most professors (beside those in colleges or schools of education) have had little to no formal training in pedagogy. Most professors rely on craft knowledge—following the examples of respected teachers, reflecting on their own teaching, and consulting colleagues about teaching issues—to develop and hone their teaching skills. (Elsewhere I have discussed deficiencies in relying on craft knowledge to resist the formal study of pedagogical theory; Speck, 2002.) Thus, those untrained to teach and probably without a self-imposed program for formally studying pedagogy consider themselves good teachers. Apparently the methods Cross's professors used to evaluate themselves were idiosyncratic, based on a professor's limited exposure to pedagogical theory and empirical studies that tested theory.

In addition, since most professors give but passing consideration to student evaluations of their teaching, claiming that such evaluations lack face validity, one pertinent source of information about professorial teaching expertise is greatly discounted. The sum of a high self-regard for one's teaching ability and low regard for students' evaluations of one's teaching is a high positive rating that generally increases with time: the longer a person teaches, the more expert he or she becomes as a teacher. Something is askew, and anyone who seeks to be an effective academic administrator will find that professorial resistance to learning how research about teaching can inform the classroom not only remains an intractable problem that hinders student learning but also presents barriers to pedagogical initiatives.

The imbalance can be righted by providing doctoral students with pedagogical training. Pedagogical training, by its very nature, entails paying careful attention to classroom management issues, and those issues are administrative concerns for both professors and administrators. For example, classroom discipline can have ramifications for academic affairs, student affairs, and financial aid. A classroom discipline issue can embroil a professor in a long string of administrative events, including informal and formal hearings with the department chair, college dean, provost, colleagues, and students impaneled on an appeals committee, and the president. A professor who wishes to prosecute successfully a case of classroom discipline needs to understand at the outset of his or her teaching career what legitimate, authorized, lawful authority he or she can claim in the classroom (Speck, 2000; Speck, 1998), and knowledge of that authority should be attained during doctoral training as part of the ordinary preparation students receive to become professional teachers.

In short, the practice of telling graduate students, either explicitly or implicitly, that the classroom is a world unto itself and the professor its prince is a false metaphor that ill serves those who aspire to success in the professoriat. Graduate students who do not understand or care to understand the interrelationships between the classroom and the entire enterprise of the university are ill prepared for the professoriat, and they could very easily find themselves embroiled in classroom situations that put them at a great disadvantage because of their ignorance of administrative procedures and requirements.

Fortunately a wealth of general sources (Brookfield, 1995; Eble, 1983; Lowman, 1995; Palmer, 1998) and specific sources (Bonwell and Eison, 1991; Cantor, 1997; Hurtdao, Milern, Clayton-Pedersen, and Allen, 1999; Johnson, Johnson, and Smith, 1991; Kurfiss, 1988; Lenning and Ebbers, 1999; Stage, Muller, Kinzie, and Simmons, 1998) about teaching is available. Anyone who graduates from a doctoral program with the intention of teaching in higher education is poorly prepared for his or her chosen occupation if courses in his or her discipline do not require interaction with that literature. Graduate students should be able to talk intelligently about foundationalism, constructivism, collaborative learning, issues related to grading, legal issues related to the classroom, technology and pedagogy, and other classroom management topics, such as syllabus preparation, learning styles, gender issues, and effective lecturing. Indeed, faculty advising of students (Kramer, 2003), an adjunct of teaching, demands a place on the list of topics with which graduate students should be conversant. I reiterate that these topics are familiar to most academic administrators because effective academic administration requires keeping current on topics related to effective teaching and advising, the problems academic administrators attempt to solve on a regular basis invariably touch on such topics, and administrators in both academic and student affairs are committed to supporting and promoting classroom teaching; and therefore they seek to understand and encourage methods that help ensure student success.

The theory of pedagogy alone, however, is insufficient. Graduate students also should be required to teach and to undergo professorial review of their teaching (Chism, 1999; Edgerton, Hutchings, and Quinlan, 1991; Hutchings, 1996, 1995). Reviewing videotapes of their classes with a mentor or professional from a teaching and learning center should be part of the graduate school experience. Graduate students who expect to teach in higher education should be required to prepare a teaching portfolio before they graduate (Anderson, 1993; Cambridge, 2001; Seldin, 1997). I say "required" because teaching is not optional for virtually all tenure-track appointments, and knowing pedagogical theory, putting that theory into practice, analyzing critiques of their classroom teaching, and preparing a portfolio that demonstrates a coherent synthesis of the theory and practice of teaching is not an unreasonable expectation for those who intend to spend their lives as professional teachers—or academic administrators.

Professors Serve. If the lack of attention to training in pedagogy at the graduate level is surprising, given that graduate programs are the font of candidates for the professoriat, no one should be caught off guard by the lack of training in how professors can serve effectively on committees. Yet committee work comprises a significant part of a professor's experience, and committee work is vital in fulfilling the goals of departments, colleges, and universities. As Smith (1981) points out, "Many service committee appointments are not a matter of choice of the faculty member. Instead, committee assignments are made on the basis of departmental and collegiate representation and many times on the social factors of cooperativeness and being known on campus" (p. 9). Woodrow (1985) notes that one of the strengths of the committee system is that "the committee can be a training ground for your faculty members and administrators" (p. 5).

I agree that the committee can be a training ground, but if craft knowledge is the basis of such on-the-job training, the success of committees will be based on the luck of the draw. As Eastwood and Tallerico (1990) found in their study of planning teams, "Respondents [team members who responded to a study of team processes] emphasized the frustration felt when teams were expected to forge into immediate action before receiving any training in the development of skills necessary to engage in successful collaborative planning and group decision making" (p. 6). Doesn't it make sense to prepare future academics for the important job of serving on committees? How can that be accomplished?

I recommend the same paradigm of theory and practice that I advocated for teaching. First, graduate students should be introduced to organizational theory regarding the academy, including literature on collaborative groups. Second, students should be assigned to committees, including stints on the academic senate.

The literature on organization theory is substantial, and its mastery would require an unreasonable effort from graduate students who do not intend to teach organizational theory, so I am not suggesting that graduate students become conversant with that body of knowledge. I am suggesting that they be introduced to the theory regarding academic organizations (Bensimon, Neumann, and Birnbaum, 1989; Bergquist, 1992; Birnbaum, 1988; Green 1988b, 1988c; Mashland, 1985; Tierney, 1988, 1990), including shared decision making (Bensimon, 1991; Mortimer and McConnell, 1978; Neumann, 1991; Powers and Powers, 1984; Yamada, 1991). In fact, the literature on collaborative group work in the classroom could be consulted profitably to gain insights into group processes (Ewald and MacCallum, 1990; Flower and Ackerman, 1994; Flower, Wallace, Norris, and Burnett, 1994; George, 1984; Higgins, Flower, and Petraglia, 1990; Hulbert, 1994; Jehn, 1997; Nelson and Smith, 1990; Plowman, 1993). That literature, which is taken largely from publications on collaborative writing (Speck, Johnson, Dice, and Heaton, 1999), is especially useful because groups are often called on to produce documents recommending certain actions. (The study of literature on collaborative writing has a potential double effect: informing graduate students about an effective classroom pedagogy and about techniques that can be adapted in administrative contexts.)

In concert with providing students a theoretical perspective on committees, doctoral programs also should require students to serve as a committee member and reflect on their service, for example, through keeping a journal, writing a paper about some aspect of committees that intrigues them, or interviewing committee members and reporting the results of those interviews. Faculty senates could foster such service by establishing internships on the senate for graduate students.

Committee work is essential in achieving the goals of the university, and achieving those goals is linked to committees' decision-making process. As Julius, Baldridge, and Pfeffer (1999) observe of universities, "Decision is by committee. Because experts, not hierarchical office, are the organizing principle, then committees of experts [but not necessarily experts in the issues a committee addresses] decide many of the critical issues" (p. 2). Thus, Woodrow (1985) is correct when he says, "College committees provide more people with the opportunity to participate in the decision-making process" (p. 2). He also notes a strength of committees: "Good committees can encourage coordination and the spirit of cooperation among departments by dealing with each other's problems. Better coordination between departments can bridge the fragmentation that occurs between today's administrative and academic specialists" (p. 3).

For all the potential good committees can achieve, we might expect that a committee member who performs well would be rewarded accordingly. Unfortunately, Boyer's assessment (1996) of the value allotted to committee work at tenure and promotion time holds true: "Almost every college catalog in this country still lists teaching, research, and service as the priorities of the professoriat; yet, at tenure and promotion time, the harsh truth is that service is hardly mentioned. And even more disturbing, faculty who do spend time with so-called applied projects frequently jeopardize their careers" (p. 13).

Graduate students should be told both the inestimable value of good committee work in promoting the institution's goals and the low rate of return placed on that work during retention, tenure, and promotion reviews. Those dual and seemingly contradictory truths will prepare them to make wise choices not only as professors but also as administrators when they ask professors to serve on committees.

Professors Are Colleagues. All that I have said in advocating a plan for addressing the "us versus them" mentality between faculty and administrators assumes that the participants in the academy endorse collegiality. However, as Bergquist (1992) points out, "Many faculty and administrators enter American colleges and universities precisely because they wish to be left alone to pursue their own teaching, research, writing, or ideas" (p. 170). Fellowes (2003), in comparing his career as a professor followed by an executive position in business, says, "For most of my academic career I had been an independent contractor. Entering the business world, I began to appreciate that most of the world's work is not done by individuals, but rather by organizations, with individuals complexly interacting and fractionally contributing to the completion of shared tasks" (p. B16). Two things strike me about Fellowes's remarks. First, as a professor, he was not an independent contractor, but his assertion that he was is made with the matter-of-factness that characterizes an attitude of independence and "autonomy" all too common in the professoriat. Second, the contrast between his self-perceived status as a professor and the typical way work gets accomplished in most organizations highlights the idiosyncratic nature of professorial self-perception and provides evidence to support the contention that professors often have difficulty understanding the need for collegiality throughout the entire academy and may even believe that collegiality works against their vested interests.

On the one hand, pronounced tensions between professors' self-interests and the requirement for collegiality are entirely understandable. Graduate students survive by stroking professors' egos in various ways. The politics of graduate education—pleasing professors to ensure that they support the graduate student—acculturates graduate students, enabling them to learn how to accommodate to power so that they can attain the acceptance that leads to the assumption of professorial power. This cycle of submission, acceptance, and elevation remains unbroken, in part, because of the kind of people who are attracted to life in the academy. For instance, in talking about the culture wars in English departments, Krupnick (2002) observes, "The hunger for social status has always seemed to me more pronounced in English professors than in other academics" (p. B16). Indeed, Krupnick notes, "English professors continue to seem to feel as if they are uniquely responsible for the spiritual condition of the nation," but their "moralism strikes me as being at odds with their obsession with the intradepartmental power plays and their rapt attention to new fashions in criticism and whatever will advance their causes" (p. B16). English professors, may I add, although exceptional specimens of attitudes that militate against collegiality, are joined by equally stark representatives of failed collegiality in other disciplines. If attacks against collegiality were limited to English departments, lack of collegiality in the academy could be contained and perhaps solved, but, in fact, we seem to perpetuate a lack of collegiality by inappropriately nurturing the ambition of graduate students in a variety of disciplines who fit our model of professional self-importance—the independent contractor lie that passes as unvarnished and unquestionable truth.

On the other hand, collegiality is a requirement for retention, tenure, and promotion. Occasionally, the *Chronicle of Higher Education* prints an article about an untenured professor who was loved by students and well published, yet was not awarded tenure or was awarded tenure after herculean struggles. The details of any particular case, often labeled an "embattled tenure case," are not germane here. What is germane is the fact that a tenure decision hung by the thread of collegiality. Why collegiality is given such importance often puzzles academics who have been led to believe that publications and excellent teaching should be the gold standard for a lifetime appointment to an academic post. Such puzzlement only serves to authenticate the independent contractor mentality that works against the good of the academy as a whole. In fact, "Courts have concluded that collegiality is implicitly embodied in considerations of the traditional criteria of teaching, research, and service. . . . The courts have affirmed at every turn the use of collegiality as a factor in making decisions concerning faculty employment, promotion, tenure, and termination, usually because of the recognition that collegiality is an important factor in the ability of colleges and universities to fulfill their missions" (Connell and Savage, 2001, p. 858).

Even if the legal status of collegiality as a bona-fide criterion for employment in the academy was not guaranteed, collegiality—the ability to promote the mission of the academy in its fullest sense—is vital for two reasons. First, collegiality is a humane requirement of those who purport to seek the good of humanity through the assiduous study of existing knowledge and the increase of that knowledge. Second, collegiality makes eminent sense. The long-term success of an organization requires that the members of the organization work in concert. As Fellowes (2003) observed, "Most of the world's work is not done by individuals, but rather by organizations, with individuals complexly interacting and fractionally contributing to the completion of shared tasks" (p. 816).

How might graduate programs incorporate both the theory and practice of collegiality into the curriculum? First, require students to read Connell and Savage's article (1991), which provides arguments for and against collegiality as a job requirement for professors and cites court cases that have been instrumental in framing legal opinions about collegiality in the academy. Second, ensure that graduate students mix with people outside their department (for example, take a course in another department, attend social activities for graduate students and faculty jointly sponsored and funded with other departments, or assume cross-disciplinary teaching assistantships). Third, analyze your department's collegiality by including graduate students in the analysis, and find ways to address lapses in collegiality.

I do not want to leave the impression that lack of collegiality is easy to solve, especially regarding tenured faculty. However, I do want to leave the impression that lack of collegiality should not be encouraged and tolerated. A significant amount of an academic administrator's time can be spent on faculty members who are not good colleagues, and problems with collegiality generally are not isolated to one or two people but have a rippling effect, washing over, sometimes as a tidal wave, the lives of many people—inside and outside the campus. Collegiality is a concern for the entire academy, but the responsibility for resolving issues related to failed collegiality lands in the administrator's office—the place where professor and administrator meet to attempt to solve collegiality problems.

Possible Objections

I foresee three objections to my proposal to include training in pedagogy, service, and collegiality in doctoral programs. The first objection will be that my proposal is unrealistic given the already crowded curriculum. There simply is no time for including such training. My answer to this objection is similar to the answer I gave colleagues when I conducted writing-across-the-curriculum seminars. Once I explained the writing process and my colleagues understood the time commitment necessary to nurture effective student writing, they frequently responded, "I can't do it. I have to teach students all the content required in my course. They have to know certain things to be successful in other courses, and I see no way to cut back on the content required." I responded, "Then don't complain about the quality of student writing. Cease blaming English departments for their introductory efforts to teach students writing skills now that you know those efforts, to be successful across the curriculum, require your support to reinforce the writing process in your courses. And now that I've provided evidence that writing is a splendid way to encourage critical thinking, please don't criticize your students anymore for their writing or thinking. Indeed, resist from criticizing any of the students at this institution whose professors are so concerned about content that writing, a proven way to enable students to master the concepts you claim are vital, is not given sufficient room in your curriculum." My response to professors who claim that graduate education is already too crowded with all the content students need to master to be effective professors is similar. We know that the professoriat requires skills in research, teaching, service, and collegiality, so if you are unwilling to include the theory and practice of the full-orbed professorial life, do not criticize your colleagues when they fail your expectations, either before or after the tenure process. (Voting against a candidate on anything but his or her publication record would be inconsistent with the philosophy that graduate education should focus on content to the virtual exclusion of teaching, service, and collegiality.) If you expect tenure-track professors to be effective teachers, your expectations must be based on an appeal to a model that supports magic. Somehow (and here is where to insert a magical formula) professors just know how to teach, serve, and be good colleagues. The history of the academy suggests that the seemingly commonsense proposition that either professors or professors in training should just know certain things about being professors is illusionary.

The second objection, akin to the first, is that graduate education is not the place to teach aspirants to the professoriat about all aspects of professorial life and especially not the relationship to administrative roles. Graduate education properly should focus on scholarship. Graduate students, if they are astute, can pick up sufficient knowledge about teaching, service, and collegiality to be successful once they are hired on the tenure track. "Many people," an objector might say, "have been successful as professors without a graduate education that included the training you deem necessary to 'the full-orbed professorial life.'"

The status quo (and elitist) argument I have just invoked disregards entirely the monumental changes in higher education that have occurred in the last sixty years, beginning with the GI Bill, continuing with open admissions in the 1960s, and reverberating today with the advent of on-line classes. What was assumed as adequate preparation for university students, a select group of people before the GI Bill and open admissions, before affirmative action and national debate about access, no longer suffices. In short, the status quo argument is based on a wistful view of the academy that has long been relegated to elite schools that have a highly selective student body. In addition, the status quo view is isolationistic in that it takes no heed of cries for accountability, yearly double-digit tuition increases that put more of the cost for education on students' (and parents') shoulders and encourages a consumer mentality and the attendant insistence that students should have a larger role in the teaching-learning enterprise, and a significant body of research that proposes ways professors can aid students in learning. I suspect that the proponent of the status quo position also says, "My job is to teach. The students' job is to learn," a bifurcated statement that lacks a logical base and divorces entirely the teaching-learning enterprise.

The third objection I foresee is that even if my proposal were enacted and even if one three-hour graduate course were carved out of the curriculum for the topics of teaching, service, and collegiality, the course would be so superficial that graduate students would not gain the type of preparation for the professoriat or academic administrative roles that I envision. Besides, who would teach such a multidisciplinary course?

Let us assume that a three-hour course is all that can be devoted to teaching graduate students about the full-orbed professorial life. I recommend that students help teach the class by reading articles and giving reports on them, not an uncommon practice in graduate classes, thus extending the coverage of materials for the course. Professors from psychology and business could serve as guest lecturers to discuss organizational theory. Professors from education could serve as guest lecturers to discuss pedagogical theory. In fact, one three-hour course for all graduate students across the disciplines creates economies of scale for teaching load credit, can become a venue for promoting interdisciplinary collegiality, and opens the possibility for exceptional graduate students in psychology, business, and education to teach their colleagues about organizational theory and pedagogy. Clearly such a course would be introductory, and I recognize the limits of attempting to address the full-orbed professorial life in a three-hour graduate course. Nevertheless, such a course would be a significant step beyond what we now do in most institutions to prepare graduate students to be successful professors with administrative duties and, for those who choose to or are chosen to serve in full-time administrative appointments, to be successful as administrators.

Conclusion

I conclude with a quotation from Tolstoy (1952) to assure my readers that I have no illusions about the possibility of preparing academics to produce "the answer" for particular administrative dilemmas. What Tolstoy describes as the difference between the theory of being a commander in chief and the actual responsibilities of a commander in chief is applicable to the academic administrator:

> The activity of a commander in chief does not at all resemble the activity we imagine to ourselves when we sit at ease in our studies examining some campaign on the map, with a certain number of troops on this and that side in a certain known locality, and begin our plans from some given moment. A commander in chief is always in the midst of a series of shifting events and so he never can at any moment consider the whole import of an event that is occurring. Moment by moment the event is imperceptibly shaping itself, and at every moment of this continuous, uninterrupted shaping of events the commander in chief is in the midst of a most complex play of intrigues, worries, contingencies, authorities, projects, counsels, threats, and deceptions and is continually obliged to reply to innumerable questions addressed to him, which constantly conflict with one another [p. 471].

Thus, training in academic administration should emphasize the complexity of the day-to-day dynamics with which academic administrators contend. If doctoral programs continue to neglect such training, we will perpetuate a grave disservice to graduate students, failing to prepare them to be successful in the varied responsibilities they will face as professors.

References

Anderson, E. (ed.). *Campus Use of the Teaching Portfolio.* Washington, D.C.: American Association for Higher Education, 1993.

Bean, J. C., and Peterson, D. "Grading Classroom Participation." In R. S. Anderson and B. W. Speck (eds.), *Changing the Way We Grade Student Performance: Classroom Assessment and the New Learning Paradigm.* New Directions for Teaching and Learning, no. 74. San Francisco: Jossey-Bass, 1998.

Bensimon, E. M. "How College Presidents Use Their Administrative Teams: 'Real' and 'Illusionary' Teams." *Journal of Higher Education Management,* 1991, 7, 35–51.

Bensimon, E. M., Neumann, A., and Birnbaum, R. *Making Sense of Administrative Leadership: The "L" Word in Higher Education.* Washington, D.C.: Association for the Study of Higher Education, 1989.

Bergquist, W. H. *The Four Cultures of the Academy: Insights and Strategies for Improving Leadership in Collegiate Organizations.* San Francisco: Jossey-Bass, 1992.

Birnbaum, R. *How Colleges Work: The Cybernetics of Academic Organizations and Leadership.* San Francisco: Jossey-Bass, 1988.

Bonwell, C. C., and Eison, J. A. *Active Learning: Creating Excitement in the Classroom.* Washington, D.C.: George Washington University, Graduate School of Education and Human Development, 1991.

Boyer, E. L. "The Scholarship of Engagement." *Journal of Public Service and Outreach,* 1996, *1*(1), 11–20.

Brookfield, S. D. *Becoming a Critically Reflective Teacher.* San Francisco: Jossey-Bass, 1995.

Cambridge, B. (ed.). *Electronic Portfolios: Emerging Practices for Students, Faculty, and Institutions.* Washington, D.C.: American Association for Higher Education, 2001.

Cantor, J. A. *Experiential Learning in Higher Education.* Washington, D.C.: George Washington University, Graduate School of Education and Human Development, 1997.

Chism, N.V.N. *Peer Review of Teaching: A Sourcebook.* Bolton, Mass.: Anker, 1999.

Connell, M. A., and Savage, F. G. "The Role of Collegiality in Higher Education Tenure, Promotion, and Termination Decisions." *Journal of College and University Law,* 1991, *27*(4), 833–858.

Corrigan, R. A. "Presidential Leadership." *Liberal Education,* 2002, *88*(4), 6–13.

Cross, K. P. "Not *Can* But *Will* College Teaching Be Improved?" In J. A. Centra (ed.), *Renewing and Evaluating Teaching.* New Directions for Higher Education, no. 17. San Francisco: Jossey-Bass, 1977.

deWinstanley, P. A., and Bjork, R. A. "Successful Lecturing: Presenting Information in Ways That Engage Effective Processing." In D. F. Halpern and M. D. Hakel (eds.), *Applying the Science of Learning to University Teaching and Beyond.* New Directions for Teaching and Learning, no. 89. San Francisco: Jossey-Bass, 1992.

Eastwood, K. W., and Tallerico, M. "School Improvement Planning Teams: Lessons from Practice." *Planning and Changing,* 1990, *21*(1), 3–12.

Eble, K. E. *The Aims of College Teaching.* San Francisco: Jossey-Bass, 1983.

Edgerton, R., Hutchings, P., and Quinlan, K. *The Teaching Portfolio: Capturing the Scholarship in Teaching.* Washington, D.C.: American Association for Higher Education, 1991.

Ewald, H. R., and MacCallum, V. "Promoting Creative Tension Within Collaborative Writing Groups." *Bulletin of the Association for Business Communication,* 1990, *53*(2), 23–26.

Fellowes, P. "From Books to Business: The Value of a Liberal Education." *Chronicle Review,* Feb. 28, 2003, p. B16.

Fish, S. "First, Kill All the Administrators." *Chronicle Review,* Apr. 14, 2003, p. B20.

Flower, L., and Ackerman, J. *Writers at Work: Strategies for Communicating in Business and Professional Settings.* New York: Harcourt Brace, 1994.

Flower, L., Wallace, D. L., Norris, L., and Burnett, R. E. (eds.). *Making Thinking Visible: Writing, Collaborative Planning, and Classroom Inquiry.* Urbana, Ill.: National Council of Teachers of English, 1994.

George, D. "Working with Peer Groups in the Composition Classroom." *College Composition and Communication,* 1984, *35*(3), 320–326.

Green, M. F. (ed.). *Leaders for a New Era: Strategies for Higher Education.* New York: American Council on Education and Macmillan, 1988a.

Green, M. F. "Leaders and Their Development." In M. F. Green (ed.), *Leaders for a New Era: Strategies for Higher Education.* New York: American Council on Education and Macmillan, 1988b.

Green, M. F. "Toward a New Leadership Model." In M. F. Green (ed.), *Leaders for a New Era: Strategies for Higher Education.* New York: American Council on Education and Macmillan, 1988c.

Grunert, J. *The Course Syllabus: A Learning-Centered Approach.* Bolton, Mass.: Anker, 1997.

Higgins, L., Flower, L., and Petraglia, J. "Planning Text Together: The Role of Critical Reflection in Student Collaboration." Paper presented at the annual meeting of the American Educational Research Association, Boston, 1990. (ED 322 495)

Hobson, E. H. "Designing and Grading Written Assignments." In R. S. Anderson and B. W. Speck (eds.), *Changing the Way We Grade Student Performance: Classroom Assessment and the New Learning Paradigm.* New Directions for Teaching and Learning, no. 74. San Francisco: Jossey-Bass, 1998.

Huber, R. M. *How Professors Play the Cat Guarding the Cream.* Fairfax, Va.: George Mason University Press, 1992.

Hulbert, J. E. "Developing Collaborative Insights and Skills." *Bulletin of the Association for Business Communication,* 1994, 57(2), 53–56.

Hurtdao, S., Milern, J., Clayton-Pedersen, A., and Allen, W. *Enacting Diverse Learning Environments.* Washington, D.C.: George Washington University, Graduate School of Education and Human Development, 1999.

Hutchings, P. *From Idea to Prototype: The Peer Review of Teaching (a Project Workbook).* Washington, D.C.: American Association for Higher Education, 1995.

Hutchings, P. *Making Teaching Community Property: A Menu for Peer Collaboration and Peer Review.* Washington, D.C.: American Association for Higher Education, 1996.

Jehn, K. A. "A Qualitative Analysis of Conflict Types and Dimensions in Organizational Groups." *Administrative Science Quarterly,* 1997, 42, 530–557.

Johnson, D. W., Johnson, R. T., and Smith, K. A. *Cooperative Learning: Increasing College Faculty Instructional Productivity.* Washington, D.C.: George Washington University, Graduate School of Education and Human Development, 1991.

Julius, D. J., Baldridge, J. V., and Pfeffer, J. "A Memo from Machiavelli." *Journal of Higher Education,* 1999, 70(2), 113–133.

Kramer, G. L. (ed.). *Faculty Advising Examined.* Bolton, Mass.: Anker, 2003.

Krupnick, M. "Why Are English Departments Still Fighting the Culture Wars?" *Chronicle Review,* Sept. 20, 2002, p. B16.

Kurfiss, J. G. *Critical Thinking: Theory, Research, Practice, and Possibilities.* Washington, D.C.: George Washington University, Graduate School of Education and Human Development, 1988.

Lenning, O., and Ebbers, L. *The Powerful Potentials of Learning Communities.* Washington, D.C.: George Washington University, Graduate School of Education and Human Development, 1999.

Lowman, J. *Mastering the Techniques of Teaching.* (2nd ed.) San Francisco: Jossey-Bass, 1995.

Mashland, A. T. "Organizational Culture in the Study of Higher Education." *Review of Higher Education,* 1985, 8, 157–168.

Mortimer, K. P., and McConnell, T. R. *Sharing Authority Effectively: Participation, Interaction, and Discretion.* San Francisco: Jossey-Bass, 1978.

Nelson, S. J., and Smith, D. C. "Maximizing Cohesion and Minimizing Conflict in Collaborative Writing Groups." *Bulletin of the Association for Business Communication,* 1990, 53(2), 59–62.

Neumann, A. "The Thinking Team: Toward a Cognitive Model of Administrative Teamwork in Higher Education." *Journal of Higher Education,* 1991, 62(5), 485–513.

Palmer, P. *The Courage to Teach: Exploring the Inner Landscape of a Teacher's Life.* San Francisco: Jossey-Bass, 1998.

Plowman, L. "Tracing the Evolution of a Co-Authored Text." *Language and Communication,* 1993, 13(3), 149–161.

Powers, D. R., and Powers, M. E. "How to Orchestrate Participatory Strategies Planning Without Sacrificing Momentum." *Educational Record,* 1984, 49, 48–52.

Quigley, B. L. "Designing and Grading Oral Communication Assignments." In R. S. Anderson and B. W. Speck (eds.), *Changing the Way We Grade Student Performance: Classroom Assessment and the New Learning Paradigm.* New Directions for Teaching and Learning, no. 74. San Francisco: Jossey-Bass, 1998.

Saroyan, A. "The Lecturer: Working with Large Groups." In J. L. Bass and others (eds.), *Teaching Alone, Teaching Together: Transforming the Structure of Teams for Teaching.* San Francisco: Jossey-Bass, 2000.

Seldin, P. *The Teaching Portfolio: A Practical Guide to Improve Performance and Promotion/Tenure Decisions.* (2nd ed.) Bolton: Anker, 1997.

Smith, G. "Applied Communication: Use of Speech Communication Faculty Expertise in University Administration." Paper presented at the annual meeting of the Southern Speech Communication Association, Austin, Tex., 1981. (ED 199 796)

Smith, K. A. "Grading Cooperative Projects." In R. S. Anderson and B. W. Speck (eds.), *Changing the Way We Grade Student Performance: Classroom Assessment and the New Learning Paradigm.* New Directions for Teaching and Learning, no. 74. San Francisco: Jossey-Bass, 1998.

Speck, B. W. "The Teacher's Role in the Pluralistic Classroom." *Perspectives,* 1998, 28(1), 19–43.

Speck, B. W. *Grading Students' Classroom Writing: Issues and Strategies.* Washington, D.C.: George Washington University, Graduate School of Education and Human Development, 2000.

Speck, B. W. "Learning-Teaching-Assessment Paradigms and the On-Line Classroom." In A. S. Anderson, J. F. Bauer, and B. W. Speck (eds.), *Assessment Strategies for the On-Line Class: From Theory to Practice.* New Directions for Teaching and Learning, no. 91. San Francisco: Jossey-Bass, 2002.

Speck, B. W., Johnson, T. R., Dice, C. P., and Heaton, L. B. *Collaborative Writing: An Annotated Bibliography.* Westport, Conn.: Greenwood Press, 1999.

Stage, F. K., Muller, P. A., Kinzie, J., and Simmons, A. *Creating Learning Centered Classrooms: What Does Learning Theory Have to Say?* Washington, D.C.: George Washington University, Graduate School of Education and Human Development, 1998.

Tierney, W. G. "Organizational Cultures in Higher Education." *Journal of Higher Education,* 1988, 59, 2–21.

Tierney, W. G. (ed.). *Assessing Academic Climates and Cultures.* New Directions for Institutional Research, no. 68. San Francisco: Jossey-Bass, 1990.

Tolstoy, L. *War and Peace* (L. Maude and A. Maude, trans.). Chicago: Encyclopedia Britannica, 1952.

Vesilind, P. A. *So You Want to Be a Professor? A Handbook for Graduate Students.* Thousand Oaks, Calif.: Sage, 2000.

Woodrow, J. *The Committee Revisited.* 1985. (ED 262 689)

Yamada, M. M. "Joint Big Decision Committees and University Governance." In R. Birnbaum (ed.), *Faculty in Governance: The Role of Senates and Joint Committees in Academic Decision Making.* New Directions for Higher Education, no. 75. San Francisco: Jossey-Bass, 1991.

BRUCE W. SPECK is professor of English and vice president for academic affairs at Austin Peay State University in Clarksville, Tennessee.

6

Faculty members desiring administrative roles can find the structure and function of shared governance a fertile ground for growth through practical experience in institutional decision making.

Faculty Governance and Effective Academic Administrative Leadership

Susan Whealler Johnston

Few new faculty are prepared by their graduate studies to participate effectively in faculty governance. In fact, many arrive at their first jobs unaware of the demands for time and political sophistication that governance may place on them. Those teaching at small, private colleges may find they are expected to participate in institution-wide committees almost immediately. Those at larger private or state universities may find themselves involved in faculty unions or elections to senates. Most will find themselves participating in departmental committee work. This often unanticipated obligation to participate in faculty governance can quickly become a burden when faculty are preparing new courses, developing research agendas, and getting to know students and departmental colleagues. As a result of competing demands on time, new faculty typically make governance a low priority, and if service to the institution through participation in governance is not rewarded in the tenure and promotion process, there is very little incentive for faculty to give this aspect of professional life much attention. The prevalence of this situation in the academy is evidenced by the number of articles, books, and conference sessions over the past several decades addressing the lack of faculty engagement in governance and the resulting lack of leadership development among faculty.

For those interested in positions within academic administration, however, understanding and participating in faculty governance is important. Academic administrative leaders are most effective when they understand and value academic culture and governance and can apply their understanding within the context of the institution's mission, its organizational needs, and its overall governance structure. They understand the relation between academic decision making and organizational decision making, as well as the process by which decisions are made at various levels within an institution. (For a helpful discussion of the distinctions between academic and organizational decision making, see Morrill, 2002.) Although good decision making is a crucial component of effective academic administration, decision making within a college or university is often no simple act. Because decisions are made through governance activities, those interested in helping faculty develop as academic leaders should find ways to help them understand institutional governance structures and engage in faculty governance at their institutions. Those administrators interested in developing their own academic leadership should pay special attention to the relation between faculty governance and other governance structures of their institutions.

Decision Making Within Colleges and Universities

Colleges and universities operate through a system of decision-making groups assigned various areas of responsibility and different levels of authority. Faculty governance is part of this institutional system of decision making. Each institution has its own faculty governance structure, as described in constitutions and by-laws and rising from its own history and culture. Some faculties, especially in smaller institutions, meet as a whole to conduct their business, while others elect representatives to carry out their work. Despite these individual differences, the vast majority of four-year institutions in the United States—over 90 percent—have some formal structure for faculty governance (Tierney and Minor, 2003).

To be effective leaders, academic administrators need to see faculty governance as one component of an institution's entire governance structure. Departments, programs, divisions or schools, campuswide committees, administration, and boards of trustees all have a role to play in an institution's governance, and if an institution is part of a state system, there are additional components in the governance structure. The level of governance decision making most familiar to a new faculty member may be the work of the department—decisions about individual courses and requirements for majors, for instance. At the departmental level, the decision-making process may be informal, controlled more by custom than constitution. As the area for decision making becomes broader (the undergraduate curriculum, graduation requirements, or admission standards, for instance) and more significant to the institution as a whole (such as the institution's budget, long-term plan, or mission), the authority for decision making changes as well, and the process generally becomes more formal.

Faculty Participation in Institutional Decision Making

What are typical areas of faculty governance work? In addition to the departmental and degree-level curricular matters, there are policies on such matters as reappointment, tenure and promotion, and academic policies for student enrollment, dismissal, and graduation, as well as assessment and program review. Some institutions include among the work of the faculty long-range academic planning and resource allocation for educational programs. Committees within departments or schools or committees of the faculty as a whole may initially address these matters—studying various sides of an issue, exploring alternatives, preparing proposals, debating strengths and weaknesses—but eventually the matters come before the faculty governing body for action. By participating in the process at the committee level, faculty—new faculty, in particular—can become familiar with issues of professional and institutional importance, educational concerns and trends, and the nature of the governance process and faculty deliberation peculiar to the institution. For instance, in a discussion of altering a general education requirement, they can learn the details of the process for curricular change, as well as national trends in undergraduate education, technical issues related to program assessment and faculty workload, the attitudes of more experienced faculty toward general education, the finesse required to run a productive meeting, and the political skills required to gather support for a particular position. Depending on the matter being discussed, the faculty member may be able to observe what happens to a recommendation when it leaves a department, a committee, or the faculty and what is done to ensure its success at its final destination—for instance, the institution's board of trustees. In addition, the faculty member may be able to learn whether the administration regularly is involved in matters of curriculum, whether the board ever rejects a plan that has been approved by the faculty, and if so, why.

Faculty Governance

For a faculty member interested in an administrative position, participating in faculty governance helps develop an awareness of the process and politics necessary to be an effective academic leader. It can offer a glimpse into the institutional governance system as a whole and the relationships among the work and concerns of faculty, administration, and board. It can also help the faculty member develop an understanding of academic culture as it is expressed at the institution.

Birnbaum (1991) describes four functions provided by faculty governance: contributing to the management of a college or university, providing a forum for faculty debate and resolution of institutional policies, developing a shared understanding of or consensus among faculty on educational or institutional goals, and symbolizing commitment to professional values and authority. For decades, there has been healthy debate (as well as no small number of jokes) about the effectiveness of faculty senates in fulfilling their responsibilities, but faculty governance continues to hold a significant position in the institutional decision-making process. In fact, a 2003 survey of faculty governance found that faculty have substantial influence on decisions in a number of areas, including curriculum, faculty personnel issues, and standards for teaching and academic quality (Tierney and Minor, 2003). Thus, despite whatever flaws there may be in the functioning of individual faculty governance bodies, it is important for institutions to support both the system of faculty governance and the constructive introduction of new faculty to the system.

Merely understanding the mechanisms of faculty governance does not make an academic administrator an effective leader. Valuing the role, symbolic as well as practical, of faculty governance within the institution's system for decision making is also important, as are the trust and respect of colleagues, support of the institutional mission, and personal integrity, among other characteristics. A good academic administrator understands academic culture and can translate that culture to others, such as board members and those outside the institution. But without respect for the faculty's distinctive professional contributions to institutional decision making and the ability to work with faculty governance to achieve desired ends, an academic administrator's success will be limited.

Shared Governance

Important in understanding how to work with faculty governance is knowing the documents, such as constitutions and by-laws, that codify and describe faculty authority in institutional decision making. Also important is knowing the various levels at which decision making occurs, from departmental to divisional, school, or college levels, from faculty to administration to board, as well as the authority assigned to the levels. This last point may well be the most difficult of all to understand fully. The term *shared governance* is applied to the process that connects and holds in balance the governance structures contributing to institutional decision making. The American Association of University Professors' 1966 *Statement on Government of Colleges and Universities* formalizes shared governance as central to the distinctive nature of American higher education and outlines those areas typically reserved for faculty responsibility. Morrill (2002) reframes the idea by referring to "collaborative governance" and arguing for faculty, administration, and board to work together to reach strategic goals and address an institution's needs for effective decision making, while preserving faculty authority in areas such as curriculum and academic standards. The devil, as always, is in the details, and it is no easy task to determine in every situation where a faculty's traditional prerogative ends and a board's legal responsibility begins. Tierney and Minor's 2003 survey on academic governance found that while the idea of shared governance is widely supported at four-year colleges and universities, there is considerable disagreement over what the term means and how it is practiced. Despite this confusion, shared governance is a fact of higher education decision making that effective academic administrators need to understand and respect. This balance of powers functions best when those with authority exercise it in the best interest of the institution and with respect for others engaged in and affected by the process.

Some Practical Suggestions

How can academic administrators help faculty understand governance so they can function effectively within it and put their understanding to good use as they move into administrative positions themselves? Here are a few practical suggestions:

• Among the criteria for tenure and promotion, make sure the institution recognizes and rewards effective service on committees (departmental, college or school, institution-wide) and in the faculty senate. It will be hard, if not impossible, to encourage faculty to devote time to faculty governance if it is not valued.

• Provide all entering faculty with an overview of the institution's governance structure and activities. Include in faculty orientation discussion of academic governance and the professional right and obligation to participate in it. Making the work of governance—at all levels—clear from the beginning of a faculty member's service increases the likelihood that he or she will take this obligation seriously.

• Make sure that information on Robert's Rules of Order is available to faculty. It is the key to appropriate participation in formal governance bodies.

• Consider providing a governance mentor for new faculty—someone who will talk candidly and helpfully about the work of governance at various levels in the institution and provide suggestions of appropriate involvement (Hamilton, 2000).

• Appoint faculty members to institution-wide committees, whether ad hoc or standing. Committees working on budgets and long-range plans are perfect places for interested faculty to see governance in action and to enlarge their view of the institution beyond the classroom and department. This important activity can help faculty develop insight into the institution's direction and goals, its relation to the world of higher education, and its place in the community, state, or region. Birnbaum (1991) refers to the faculty senate as a "personnel screening device" (p. 17), providing academic administrators opportunities to see faculty in action and help them understand the values of the institution. Institution-wide committees can function in the same way.

• Regularly attend meetings of the faculty senate or governing body. Attending these meetings shows respect for the work done there and can provide an opportunity to hear from faculty, in their own voices, what they are working on or concerned about.

• Communicate regularly with the faculty about actions taken on matters for which their committees or senate provided information, suggestions, or votes. This helps faculty understand their governance contributions in the larger context of the institution.

• Regularly share important institutional information so that participation in governance is not about being on the inside but rather about service to the profession and the institution.

• If appropriate, suggest that faculty attend open meetings of the board. For private institutions, this might mean a meeting of the academic affairs committee of the board of trustees. For public institutions, this could mean attending any of the open meetings of the full board.

• Provide opportunities for faculty to meet with administrators and board members. Social occasions, committee meetings, and open discussions can help faculty members understand the larger governance picture of the institution.

• Suggest that governance documents be reviewed regularly if this is not currently done. This can provide opportunities for new voices to be heard on matters of faculty governance, and it can ensure that important new issues are addressed.

• Make sure there is an intentional, practical system for leadership succession within faculty governance. For instance, is the process for obtaining leadership positions within, such as the faculty senate, well defined? Are there processes in place to allow new academic leaders to benefit from the experience of previous leaders?

• Take faculty governance seriously. A good academic administrator understands faculty governance and culture. Although faculty governance may not always work as smoothly and efficiently as one might wish, it is an integral part of an institution's decision-making structure. Taking it seriously does not mean always following the recommendations coming from it, but it does mean respecting the role faculty and faculty governance play in the institution. The list of "Traits of Effective Senates" (Flynn, 2000) is a helpful starting place in reviewing and strengthening an institution's faculty governance.

Conclusion

Participation in faculty governance is not a natural act, especially given the specialized academic study required to become a faculty member and the competing demands placed on faculty members. Nonetheless, it is important for those interested in academic administration. A grounding in the structure, function, and distinctive nature of faculty governance is critical for any faculty member who may become a dean, provost, or president and needs to work with and through leaders of faculty governing bodies. It lends credibility, affords insight into institutional decision making, and develops a more comprehensive view of an institution.

Governance responsibilities of academic institutions are often ambiguous, and the work can be time-consuming and fraught with political difficulties. However, there is no doubt about the consequence inherent in this work. An institution's nature, shape, and future are determined as a result of governance activity. For those interested in academic administration at any level, thoughtful participation in and reflection on faculty governance can be a key to more successful leadership in the future.

References

American Association of University Professors. *Statement on Government of Colleges and Universities.* Washington, D.C.: American Association of University Professors, 1966.

Birnbaum, R. "The Latent Organizational Functions of the Academic Senate: Why Senates Do Not Work But Will Not Go Away." In R. Birnbaum (ed.), *Faculty in Governance: The Role of Senates and Joint Committees in Academic Decision Making.* New Directions for Higher Education, no. 75. San Francisco: Jossey-Bass, 1991.

Flynn, J. *Traits of Effective Senates.* 2000. [www.aaup.org/governance/resources/ttr-raits.htm].

Hamilton, N. "The Academic Profession's Leadership Role in Shared Governance." *Liberal Education,* 2000, *86,* 12–19.

Morrill, R. *Strategic Leadership in Academic Affairs: Clarifying the Board's Responsibilities.* Washington, D.C.: Association of Governing Boards of Universities and Colleges, 2002.

Tierney, W., and Minor, J. *Challenges for Governance: A National Report.* Los Angeles: University of Southern California Center for Higher Education Policy Analysis, 2003.

SUSAN WHEALLER JOHNSTON is vice president for INDEPENDENT SECTOR programs at the Association of Governing Boards of Universities and Colleges.

7

The basis for sound administrative decisions in colleges and universities lies in broad-based knowledge of federal and state constitutional and statutory provisions, case law, policies of governing boards, and other legal issues affecting higher education.

Selected Legal Aspects of Academic Administrative Leadership: An Orientation for New Academic Administrators

Charles R. Jenkins

Academic administrators face the challenging responsibility of staying knowledgeable of current federal and state laws related to higher education and implementing these laws into their respective administrative duties and decisions. Specifically, academic administrators are responsible for upholding federal and state constitutional and statutory provisions, judicial decisions, and policies of governing boards; negotiating with federal and state compliance agencies; and providing academic leadership to develop and implement sound educational policies and practices. Consequently, new and prospective academic administrators, to be effective, need to understand the impact of laws governing and influencing higher education.

As the number and scope of federal statutory provisions affecting higher education have increased through the years, so have the number and complexity of legal issues in academic administration intensified. The growing litigious nature of our society has amplified the criticality for knowledge in basic legalities. We may be discouraged at times with the legal issues involved in the academic administration and in society in general, but the well-known statement by founding father John Adams that "we are a nation of laws, not men" continues to ring true.

In providing an orientation and overview for new and prospective academic leaders, this chapter is necessarily limited in scope given the enormity of higher education law. Thus, the following topics were selected for

New Directions for Higher Education, no. 124, Winter 2003 © Wiley Periodicals, Inc.

discussion: constitutional provisions, including due process; statutory provisions; federal administrative enforcement; contractual provisions; case law; policies; open meetings laws; decision making; preventive law and legal and risk audits; and resources.

Constitutional Provisions

The First and Fourteenth amendments of the U.S. Constitution have particular significance for higher education. The following paragraphs highlight the most relevant aspects of these two constitutional amendments with respect to issues that public colleges and universities face.

The First Amendment's establishment clause and free exercise clause require that public institutions remain neutral in religious matters, maintaining the separation of church and state. These clauses also require public institutions to protect, in a reasonable manner, the religious rights of students, faculty, and staff. The First Amendment's free speech clause seeks to protect the rights of students and faculty regarding various forms of expression. Courts have protected the expression rights as long as there is not "material and substantial disruption" of the institution's programs and activities (Hudgins and Vacca, 1999, p. 397). Although interpreted differently in definition, scope, and extent, the institution's and faculty's academic freedom remains viable, particularly for inquiry related to research and teaching. Despite this academic freedom, there necessarily exists an expected degree of responsibility in teaching the captive audience in the classroom as compared to an open forum. Landry (2002) concludes: "Controversial or profane in-class speech that is not germane or that constitutes a significant curricular deviation in content or methodology, is constitutionally speaking, high-risk behavior, and professors should not expect judicial protection for such utterances" (p. 25). Thus, for example, academic freedom does not protect a faculty member when it is determined that a hostile, sexually discriminatory learning environment exists in a classroom in violation of institutional policy or federal laws. Therefore, an institution can place limitations on such classroom speech as long as "the limitations are reasonable and narrowly tailored" (Zirkel, 1997, p. 478).

The Fourteenth Amendment protects the specified privileges of citizens in its due process clause and equal protection clause. The due process requirements include substantive due process (the protected privilege or right, such as freedom of speech) and procedural due process (the procedures that protect the substantive right). The equal protection clause's impact on higher education is profound, particularly in equalizing educational and employment opportunities with respect to race, national origin, sex, religion, age, and disability. Some federal laws that assist in implementing the equal protection clause by means of prohibiting discrimination and equalizing educational and employment opportunities are covered in the statutory provisions section.

Due process procedures in academic administration, including adequate notice and the opportunity to present one's side of the story, serve not only to assist an institution in meeting the legal requirements of constitutional and contractual provisions of the law, but also seek to ensure fundamental fairness. A public institution cannot deny a student or faculty or staff member a liberty or property interest without due process; usually private institutions follow similar due process procedures. It is not always clear what constitutes a liberty or property interest, and consultation with the campus attorney is advisable when in doubt.

Due process in higher education does not necessarily need to be the same as in the courts. In academic administration, the type and extent of due process is normally provided in accordance with the severity of the situation, and situations in which a liberty or property interest is not at stake can normally be handled through objective administrative review procedures. In many cases, that may basically mean the aggrieved persons are provided the opportunity to present their side of the story to the responsible authorities. If the action is academic in nature rather than disciplinary, a formal hearing may not be required. However, when a liberty or property interest is potentially being denied, due process procedures, including a more formal hearing, are usually required. Administrators must be judicious in following the Constitution's requirement for due process policies and procedures, and because these policies and procedures play such an important role in academic administration, they should be reviewed periodically with the campus attorney to ensure that they are legally sound (Stevens, 1999).

Statutory Provisions

Statutory law plays a critical role in higher education, especially with the volume and impact of federal and state legislation in education. Each state's constitution makes provisions for public higher education within that state, and therefore it is essential that administrators take the time to become familiar with those provisions. In this section, the following selected federal statutory provisions—designed to provide equal opportunity, prevent discrimination, and help implement in many situations the equal protection clause of the Fourteenth Amendment—are presented due to their importance for academic administration:

• Title VI of the Civil Rights Act of 1964 (sec. 2000 D-D-1) prohibits discrimination on the basis of race, color, or national origin in any program or activity receiving federal funds of any type and requires the termination of federal financial assistance if discrimination exists. Since most institutions of higher education receive federal funds in various forms, this provision is of significant importance to academic administration.

• Title VII of the Civil Rights Act of 1964 (sec. 2000 E-2) addresses equal employment opportunity and prohibits discrimination on the basis of race, color, religion, sex, or national origin in public and private workplaces. These comprehensive prohibitions include hiring; discharging; compensation and privileges; classifying employees or applicants; or otherwise adversely affecting an employee because of race, color, religion, sex, or national origin.

• The 1994 federal Age Discrimination in Employment Act also addresses the equal employment issue by eliminating the mandatory retirement age of seventy and prohibiting dismissal of faculty and staff members solely on the basis of age.

• Title IX of the 1972 Education Amendments Act (sec. 1681), often referred to as gender equity, specifically addresses discrimination on the basis of sex and is enforced by the termination of federal assistance. Although much media attention is given to equity in athletics for women as a result of Title IX, the breadth of this provision is more comprehensive than gender equity in athletic programs. Title IX also protects an individual from sexual harassment, quid pro quo situations, and hostile environments within the classroom or in campus programs and activities. Furthermore, harassment of students by other students (even students of the same gender) and harassment of students by faculty and staff are covered by Title IX. (Title VII of the Civil Rights Act of 1964 covers harassment in the workplace.) Consequently, both a professional and a legal responsibility requires academic administrators to follow up appropriately on reports and patterns of sexual harassment.

• The laws protecting educational opportunities for students with disabilities continue to evolve. Section 504 of the Rehabilitation Act of 1973 prohibits discrimination against "otherwise qualified individuals" and requires public institutions of higher education to remove barriers, thereby increasing accessibility. In a similar vein, the Americans with Disabilities Act (ADA) of 1990 is a comprehensive statute prohibiting discrimination against people with disabilities by both public and private employers and by institutions receiving financial assistance. This act also expands the definition of disabilities and requires that "reasonable accommodations" for people with disabilities be made (sec. 10101). The Individuals with Disabilities Act of 1992 and 1997 retitles section 504 of the Rehabilitation Act of 1973 and provides more precise definitions of disabilities and precise specifications for services intended to maximize the opportunities and services available. These laws now make it clear that the institution is required to provide a reasonable accommodation if a student indicates having a disability. After there is agreement by the institution and the student on the reasonable accommodation, faculty and staff are expected to follow through with the agreement. A campus appeals process to handle disability grievances is required legally, and appeal procedures usually involve a senior-level administrator and the campus attorney. For cases not resolved at the institutional level, the Office of Civil Rights provides an easy process for filing a grievance.

• Originally passed in 1974 and amended several times, the Family Education Rights and Privacy Act (FERPA), sometimes referred to as the Buckley Amendment, protects the privacy of students' educational records and ensures students' accessibility to those records. FERPA's definition and specifications of educational records and of directory information continue to evolve. Thus, it is imperative for academic administrators and especially registrars, working in conjunction with campus attorneys, to maintain knowledge of FERPA's most current provisions.

Federal Administrative Enforcement

The federal Equal Employment Opportunity Commission (EEOC) is the governmental agency responsible for publishing regulations and enforcing Title VII of the Civil Rights Act. This agency is also required to investigate filed charges of unlawful discrimination in the workplace, including sexual discrimination and harassment. Academic administrators are required at various times to assist in providing information and data to EEOC and to respond to filed charges upon EEOC inquiry.

The U.S. Department of Education's Office for Civil Rights (OCR) is responsible for publishing regulations for federally assisted programs and activities, including research grants, and for enforcing Title VI, Title IX, FERPA, and the disability enactments. OCR's governing responsibilities also include protections against age discrimination and sexual harassment in the classroom and in campus programs and activities.

Contractual Provisions

Public and private institutions of higher education are subject to a variety of contractual obligations, such as those explicitly stated in faculty and staff employment contracts. Public and private institutions also have implied relationships with employees and students in the form of faculty handbooks, course syllabi, college and university catalogues, student handbooks, and policy statements. Under such implied contractual relationships, employed representatives of the institution cannot make decisions about students in an arbitrary, capricious, discriminatory, or unreasonable manner. In the case of course syllabi, it is normally understood that a faculty member can make reasonable changes as deemed appropriate during a course as long as adequate notice is provided for the student to meet the changes. Placing a statement on the syllabus that clearly reserves the right of a faculty member to make appropriate changes when needed is a good practice and should be required. Furthermore, appropriate academic advisement is essential in assisting students and preventing potential legal and administrative problems that may arise from implied contractual relationships between institutions and students (Kaplin and Lee, 1995).

In contrast to public institutions, private institutions are generally governed more by contractual provisions than public laws. Nevertheless, certain statutory enactments still have significant implications for private schools. Specifically, Title VII's workplace discrimination protections are in force, and violations of Title VI and Title IX may lead to the elimination of federal support for research projects and financial aid to students (Toma and Palm, 1999).

Case Law

Lawsuits appear to be increasing on behalf of students and faculty regarding violations of the constitutional and statutory provisions previously identified, as well as regarding other legal claims. The judicial decisions and precedents established in many of these court cases can have significant implications for academic administration and may serve as an important guide for policymaking and decision making in higher education. Some of the most common and relevant cases involve aspects of academic administration, such as discrimination based on race, ethnicity, religion, gender, disabilities, and age; sexual harassment; faculty concerns, such as faculty disciplinary proceedings, academic freedom, tenure decisions and procedures; and even grades (White, 2002). Although campus attorneys will provide particular advice to academic officers regarding pertinent court cases and judicial decisions, academic officers should make an effort on their own to be well informed of these cases and decisions. And although significant differences exist between public school education and higher education, following pertinent public school cases can also provide insight into laws affecting academic administration in higher education.

Shortly before this chapter went to press, the U.S. Supreme Court ruled on perhaps the most long-term, controversial, and emotional issue in higher education: the legal status of race-conscious admissions or affirmative action. The two cases before the Supreme Court, *Gratz et al.* v. *Bollinger et al.* (2003) and *Grutter* v. *Bollinger et al.* (2003), focused on race-conscious procedures in use at the University of Michigan for undergraduate admissions and for law school admissions to promote diversity as a "compelling University interest." Both sides of the affirmative action debate claimed victory when the Court affirmed the authority of higher education institutions to consider race as one factor among many in admission decisions but qualified that consideration in terms of implementation. Importantly, the use of race or ethnicity is allowable

> where necessary to further their (universities or colleges) *compelling* interest in promoting the educational benefits of diversity. The court also held that when colleges and universities pursue this interest, only program designs that ensure individualized consideration of applicants (and their diversity attributes) can be sufficiently *narrowly tailored* to meet federal

legal requirements. Thus, the Court upheld the University of Michigan's Law School admissions policy (in *Grutter v. Bollinger et al.*), which includes an individualized, full-file review of all applications, while striking down the University of Michigan's undergraduate admissions policy (in *Gratz et al. v. Bollinger et al.*), which assigns points to applicants based on certain admissions criteria, including race and ethnicity [Coleman and Palmer, 2003, p. 1].

Much analysis remains to be done about these landmark decisions, but colleges and universities should inventory and review all race-based policies in relation to diversity goals (Coleman and Palmer, 2003).

Policies

The policies that govern all areas of academic affairs, including the employment of faculty and staff, are critical to the effective operation of colleges and universities in meeting legal provisions and requirements and in accomplishing their mission of teaching, research, and service. Governing boards develop policies that cover most of the important areas of concern, and attorneys usually assist with the legal ramifications of those policies. Academic administrators, with appropriate involvement and endorsement through a shared governance system with faculty, play an essential role in policy development and implementation and should also seek the advice of the campus attorney regarding policies that have potential legal ramifications. Developing and following through with sound written policies covering all areas of the academic operation can be a successful strategy for reducing legal problems and accomplishing the college and university mission. Regular reviews (at least annually) of institutional policies are needed for updating, improving, and ensuring that these policies are legally and administratively sound. Although revisions of policies and requirements are often necessary, students and faculty must be given adequate notice and provided fundamental fairness, including a reasonable time frame to meet such changes. In developing and reviewing policies, it can be insightful to examine comparable policies of three to five peer institutions.

One of the most challenging areas of responsibility of academic administrators is the development and implementation of policies and procedures related to appointment, promotion, and tenure of faculty. The legal implications of these particular policies and procedures can be significant. The following review points may be helpful to new academic administrators in preventing or reducing legal consequences when making decisions:

- A well-designed procedural checklist for the recruitment and selection of new faculty is essential, including appropriate data collection for affirmative action and equal opportunity documentation and other legal purposes.

• Questions and statements used in the search and interview phase should focus on the expectations, performance, expertise, and qualifications required in the position and should not pertain to the applicant's race, national origin, religion, sex, age, handicap or disabilities, sexual preference, marital or family status, and political associations.

• For probationary faculty (those who are on tenure track but have not been awarded tenure) and faculty who are not on tenure track, adequate notice of nonrenewal or renewal in accordance with institutional policy, especially regarding the time frames required, is required. For the academic officers responsible for this important process, a systematic approach designed to meet and complete the necessary timelines and procedures is essential. The probationary period provides the institution the opportunity to screen out faculty members who do not have the expertise or do not meet the standards needed by the institution in accomplishing its mission. An important question for academic officers might be whether it is appropriate to reappoint a probationary faculty member if it is largely concluded that the probationary faculty member will not be recommended for tenure. It is much better to make that difficult decision during the earlier phases of the probationary period than to wait until the final decision period—the "up or out" year. Wolverton, Gmelch, Montez, and Nies (2001) reinforce the concept that institutions have much discretion in nonreappointment and in denying tenure "except when a protected class or fundamental right is involved" (p. 61). Joyce (2000) advises that the reasons for nonreappointment or tenure denial should not be arbitrary (done nonrationally or according to decision maker's pleasure, and without adequate principle by which to decide); capricious (not based on fact or reason); discriminatory with respect to race, national origin, sex, religion, age, or disability; or for political or personal reasons. Negative decisions that are seen as being vindictive rather than based on sound rationale are unacceptable.

• Tenure supports free inquiry and academic freedom in teaching and research and protects a faculty member from dismissal for unjustified reasons. Justified reasons normally include incompetence, neglect of duty, and conviction of serious crimes. If good judgment is used and appropriate and specified procedural due process is followed, courts usually allow academic administrators reasonable discretion in the dismissal of tenured faculty for justified reasons.

• Tenured faculty have a property interest and thus are entitled to due process, which is normally detailed in the faculty handbook. Academic officers should be judicious in carrying out the due process procedures in a timely and prudent manner as specified in the policies. Failure to do so could have serious legal consequences.

• Courts are very protective of First Amendment rights, and when courts determine that a faculty member is being dismissed for exercising freedom of speech or expression, they normally side with the faculty.

However, faculty will be at risk if they abuse the responsibility that comes with classroom teaching (as already noted).

• Strengthening the faculty and staff is one of the most important responsibilities of academic officers. Therefore, the key periods that should receive a great deal of attention and effort are the search and interview phase, the reappointment or nonreappointment phase, and the tenure decision year. These three periods must be taken seriously, not only as opportunities to strengthen the faculty, but also to maintain the best standards and practices in higher education in hiring, reappointing, and awarding tenure.

Open Meetings Laws

Administrators in public institutions should be careful to adhere to the open meetings laws or policies that pertain to their institution. These state laws typically require public institutions of higher education to provide notice of and open all meetings of the governing board and its committees to the public. Meetings of the faculty and professional staff are usually excluded from such requirements. The board of trustees and its committees may normally go into closed or executive sessions, excluding those not invited to attend, to discuss the following particular limited categories of items: personnel matters, confidential information, acquisition of property, and consulting with legal counsel. Although these items may be discussed and decided in closed sessions, they usually must be officially acted on with no discussion required in open session (Joyce, 2000).

Decision Making

One of the most important functions and responsibilities of academic administration is decision making with respect to students, faculty, staff, and academic programs and activities. The decision-making process and the actual decisions themselves should be professionally and legally sound. In general, the legal system supports the concept of the faculty and administration, with particular expertise in higher education, making academic decisions. The essentials of effective decision making include good judgment, fundamental fairness, reasonableness, precedent, consistency, and common sense. Academic administrators should also have general and specific knowledge of academic programs and policies and education law. "Treating others as you would like to be treated" continues to be a good professional and ethical guide to follow in preventing and reducing legal consequences. Standards of reasonableness and fundamental fairness are generally expected in the legal structure and should be key components in word and deed in academic administration. Precedent not only plays a very important role in case law but also can play an important role in academic decision making because it promotes fairness and consistency throughout the institution. Precedents in decision making evolve, but naturally decisions are not bound by precedent when circumstances and situations warrant change. Reviewing and examining precedent strengthens decision making, but attention must be given to ensure that the circumstances and situations are truly analogous. Decisions should not be made on the basis of administrative ease or convenience.

The following decision-making model can be helpful, especially for difficult decisions: gather accurate information or the facts from the best sources possible, including pertinent legal ramifications; outline the pros and cons of each option; examine precedent in an analogous situation and the precedent you may be establishing (remembering that precedent promotes consistency and fairness throughout the institution); consult, when appropriate, with the campus attorney and supervisor; and determine the sound rationale behind the final decision. It is very important to have a legitimate rationale—both legal and ethical—for decisions, and documenting that rationale can be helpful for future reference. People will not always agree with the decisions, but if you have a sound rationale for the decision, you can defend it if challenged. In difficult situations that have legal ramifications, it may be insightful to speculate along with the campus attorney as to how the courts would perceive this situation. Examining the intent of a given policy or law can also serve instructively at times. Academic administrators have the responsibility to ensure that a balance exists between students meeting their own responsibilities and the institution living up to its responsibilities and doing what it states it will do. If there is doubt whether the institution is living up to its responsibilities, the benefit of the doubt should go to the student. Maintaining integrity and good academic standards is also an important role of academic administrators and ensuring that the institution is carrying out its responsibility is part of that process.

Preventive Law and Legal and Risk Audits

In recent years, one of the most important evolving areas or services provided by the campus attorney is in the areas known as preventive law and legal or risk audits. These audits are conducted as a preemptive way of reducing institutional liability and can provide the basis for careful planning and implementation as well as risk assessment and management. A significant benefit of risk assessment is that administrators and faculty involved in the program or activity under review develop knowledge and understanding concerning the legal issues and the pertinent laws. In addition, such audits review institutional policies, procedures, and practices for their internal consistency within the institution, for their consistency with the law, and for their reasonableness and fairness (Thomas, 1998).

One area where preventive law and legal and risk audits could be particularly beneficial is study abroad programs. These programs play a very important role in the educational mission of many institutions of higher education, but they can create challenges and risks, including institutional liability. Careful planning and implementation, as well as effective risk management, including insurance protection, can reduce problems. Academic administrators directly responsible for study abroad programs should examine the challenges and risks involved, confer with others who have successfully carried out these programs, and participate in conferences or workshops focusing on risk management related to study abroad programs (University of North Carolina at Chapel Hill, 2002).

Resources

The campus attorney should be the top resource for advising and for researching various legal issues. In addition, there are helpful selected electronic law sources for legal research (examples are http://findlaw.com; http://law.emory.edu/LAW/refdesk/toc.html; http://supt.law.cornell.edu/supct/; http://www.wrightslaw.com/law; and http://www.lexis.com). For administrators who serve in the state-supported institutions that are part of a higher education system or coordinating unit, legal counsel employed by the system office can be a very effective resource on legal issues and areas of concern, particularly because they can advise how other institutions have managed similar issues and experiences. The state attorney general's office in each state can provide assistance and legal opinions that are helpful but not binding, if requested by the president or board chair. Most states also have an agency or institute that provides legal assistance and advice to governmental entities including colleges and universities. Several other sources can be used and be most instructive, including the *Journal of Law and Education, Journal of College and University Law,* and *Chronicle of Higher Education.*

A solid publication focused on employment law is a must for all academic administrators. In addition, participation in conferences and workshops that conduct sessions on legal issues in higher education is most interesting and informative. For example, some of the most popular and best attended sessions at the annual meeting of the Commission of Colleges, Southern Association of Colleges and Schools, are those devoted to legal issues in colleges and universities. Furthermore, Thomas (1998) provides a comprehensive and valuable discussion on the attorney's role on campus, which is particularly helpful to institutions that are in the process of employing legal counsel or studying and reorganizing legal services.

Conclusion

An academic leader needs to have a basic understanding of the relevant constitutional and statutory provisions, evolving laws, and legal issues affecting higher education and the relationship between legal considerations and academic administration. At the same time, an academic leader must focus on accomplishing the goals, objectives, and highest ideals of the academy in teaching, scholarship, and service while incorporating the applicable legal considerations into policies, processes, procedures, practices, and decisions. Indeed, a close relationship exists between effective administration and developing and following policies, processes, procedures, and practices that are legally sound.

One of the most effective means that an academic administrator may use to prevent or reduce legal problems is to continuously apply basic ethical principles of the profession, such as treating others as you would like to be treated; acting in good faith; being fair-minded, consistent, and reasonable; applying good judgment, common sense, and standards of reasonableness; and not acting vindictively. Also, appropriate documentation of situations and issues that have potential legal ramifications is an essential precautionary measure as well as a mandatory measure in case of legal challenge. Furthermore, developing and maintaining a positive, helpful, and supportive working relationship with the campus or system attorney is critical for effective academic leadership and contributes to peace of mind.

Many of the challenges in academic administration will continue to include legal issues and considerations, and academic leaders should strive to maintain an up-to-date knowledge of laws and judicial decisions affecting all aspects of higher education. The threat or reality of facing a lawsuit is always present in academic administration, but academic leaders should not allow that fact to intimidate or paralyze them from providing leadership and doing what is right and best for students, faculty, staff, and the ideals of the academy.

References

Age Discrimination Act. 29 U.S. Code 1994.

Americans with Disabilities Act. 42 U.S. Code. 1990.

Civil Rights Act of 1964. 42 U.S. Code Annotated. 1964.

Coleman, A., and Palmer, S. *The U.S. Supreme Court Decision in Gratz v. Bollinger and Grutter v. Bollinger (Issued June 23, 2003). Case Analysis and Lessons Learned.* Washington, D.C.: Nixon Peabody LLP, 2003.

Education Amendment Act. 20 U.S. Code Annotated. 1972.

Family Education Rights and Privacy Act. 20 U.S. Code Annotated, Family Educational and Privacy Act. 1974.

Gratz et al. v. Bollinger et al. 123 S. Ct. 2411, June 23, 2003.

Grutter v. Bollinger et al. 123 S. Ct. 2325, June 23, 2003.

Hudgins, H. C., and Vacca, R. S. *Law and Education: Contemporary Issues and Court Decisions.* (5th ed.) New York: Lexis, 1999.

Individuals with Disabilities Education Act. 20 U.S. Code, sec. 1400–185. 1997.

Joyce, R. P. *The Law of Employment in North Carolina's Public Schools.* Chapel Hill: University of North Carolina at Chapel Hill: Institute of Government, 2000.

Kaplin, W. A., and Lee, B. A. *The Law of Higher Education.* (3rd ed.) San Francisco: Jossey-Bass, 1995.

Landry, A. "Professional Speech and Academic Freedom: Can *Hardy* v. *Jefferson Community College* Be Reconciled with *Urofsky* v. *Gilmore,* or Is There a Conflict in the Judicial View of In-Class and Other Professional Speech?" In *Proceedings of the Twenty-Third Annual Conference on Law and Higher Education.* St. Petersburg, Fla.: Stetson University College of Law, 2002.

Rehabilitation Act of 1973. 29 U.S. Code, sec. 794. sec. 504. 1973.

Stevens, E. *Due Process and Higher Education: A Systematic Approach to Fair Decision Making.* Washington, D.C.: George Washington University Graduate School of Education and Human Development, 1999.

Thomas, N. L. "The Attorney's Role on Campus." *Change,* 1998, *30*(3), 35–42.

Toma, J. D., and Palm, R. L. *The Academic Administrator and The Law: What Every Team and Department Chair Needs to Know.* Washington, D.C.: George Washington University Graduate School of Education and Human Development, 1999.

University of North Carolina at Chapel Hill. *Proceedings of Study Abroad: A Risk Audit Workshop,* Apr. 5, 2002.

White, L. "The United States Supreme Court: A Critical Review of Recent and Pending Cases That Are Likely to Have a Significant Impact on Higher Education Administration." In *Proceedings of the Twenty-Third Annual National Conference on Law and Higher Education.* St. Petersburg, Fla.: Stetson University College of Law. 2002.

Wolverton, M., Gmelch, W. H., Montez, J., and Nies, C. T. *The Changing Nature of the Academic Deanship.* Washington, D.C.: George Washington University Graduate School of Education and Human Development, 2001.

Zirkel, P. A. "Courtside: Poisons in the Halls of Ivy." *Phi Delta Kappan,* 1997, 78(6), 478–479.

CHARLES R. JENKINS is a professor of educational leadership at the University of North Carolina at Pembroke.

8

Five key features of community undergird commitment to diversity in a university or college based on the principles of servant leadership.

Promoting Diversity in Academic Leadership

Oscar C. Page

> Good leadership fosters change that is both transformative and sustainable. It can be concerned with moral or organizational matters. It can define the college's role in the world beyond its walls, or it can determine the internal dynamics of the institution. Most importantly, it requires a worthy goal—vision, if you will—but it also requires persistence.
>
> R. Ekman, 2003

Although Ekman (2003) refers to presidential leadership, his remarks relate directly to the issue of promoting diversity in academic leadership. As colleges and universities define their role and reflect on the moral and organizational aspects of their mission statements, academic administrators must have a vision not only for the basics of a curriculum and the development of a faculty but also for the composition of the student body, faculty, and administration. An effective understanding of this vision and commitment will lead to the establishment of a diverse administrative team (Diamond, 2002).

The most powerful theory of leadership that is supportive of a diverse culture is servant leadership, a theory that first came into prominence when Greenleaf (1970) published *Servant as Leader*. In fact, the Greenleaf Center for Servant Leadership has produced numerous conferences and articles on the subject. Spears (1998) discusses Greenleaf and defines servant leadership as the creation of a community that "puts serving others—including employees, customers, and community—as the number one priority"

(p. 3). Spears identifies the servant leader as one who first makes "sure that other people's highest priority needs are being served" (p. 3). He then asks the rhetorical question, "Do those served grow as persons; do they, while being served, become healthier, wiser, freer, more autonomous, more likely themselves to become servants?" (p. 3). If the institution adopts the theory that leadership must reflect the composition of the constituency and must provide a role model for other leaders, then the leader will recognize that he or she serves the needs of all those represented within the institution.

To produce a diverse community, the leadership team will be committed to five key features of the community:

1. A commitment to understanding other cultures and the value of diversity in leadership positions
2. The understanding and commitment to basic values that flow through the organization
3. The creation of a culture of trust where the diverse organization has a high level of respect for all cultures represented
4. The conscious development of strategies to recruit or provide mobility for women and ethnic minorities within the organization
5. A willingness to be accountable for the success or failure of promoting diversity within the academic leadership—accountable for monitoring and mentoring the leader

Commitment to Understanding Other Cultures

Commitment to understanding other cultures and the value of diversity within leadership is essential to the success of a leadership team within a college or university. Covey (1999) cites research by the Center for Creative Leadership that showed that "respect for the differences in people" is one of the more important qualities of a successful leader (p. 162). Of critical importance is the recognition that the large and small issues relative to culture are important to the success of the leader. The successful academic leader will "understand, appreciate, and motivate" colleagues in a variety of cultures, demonstrating the values evident in all of them (p. 162). On a college campus, it is important for the academic leader to be involved with students representing a variety of cultures by participating in activities that are important to each culture, in essence demonstrating a commitment to the understanding of the culture reflected in the mission of the college and in the lives of the students.

The first building block on which an institution can promote diversity within the academic leadership is to employ leaders who recognize that they must serve all constituents to secure followers from any constituency. Leaders must understand the culture and value diversity and, as Covey says, "have respect for the differences in people" (1999, p. 162).

Understanding and Commitment to Basic Values

The second key to promoting diversity within the academic leadership team is commitment to basic values. Embedded in those values must be a clear understanding of the multicultural dimensions of an institution that respects the traditional values of various cultures. Bordas (1995) says, "Many women, minorities, and people of color have long traditions of servant leadership in their cultures. Servant leadership has very old roots in many of the indigenous cultures, cultures that were holistic, cooperative, communal, intuitive, and spiritual" (p. 10). The cultural roots of servant leadership are grounded in the values inherent in a community and the necessity for leadership to reflect these values. If an academic leader is to be successful, he or she must believe in the values that are evident in the multicultural population of the college or university. It is not enough to include value statements in the institution's vision. It is essential to incorporate such values as respect, service, and equity into the decisions made by the administrator. Out of this will come a culture of trust.

Culture of Trust

Leaders often fail because they do not consistently work toward a culture of trust. Understanding what is meant by the values of respect, service, and equity helps to establish this culture. Respect for oneself, others, and the culture of the various individuals who are represented on campus is essential. For example, colleges and universities must provide the means for various ethnic minorities to celebrate their cultures. Whether they are Indian, African American, Asian, Native American, or Hispanic, ethnic minorities belong to cultures that embody the values of respect, service, and equity, which are demonstrated in various celebrations. Indeed, many cultures have a spiritual dimension that must be respected, and out of the spiritual dimension generally comes an understanding of serving other people. To be successful in the climate of diversity and to maintain a healthy institution, administrative decisions must reflect a true understanding of the values of respect, service, and equity that are embodied in the culture of the diverse groups represented on campus.

A commitment to understanding other cultures and the basic values reflected in the various cultures is a critical step in establishing a culture of trust. Bordas (1995) asks, "Whom does the servant leader serve?" She answers this question by drawing on the principles expressed by Greenleaf, but she takes the answer a step further and says, "Just as a servant leader is a servant first and begins with a natural feeling that one wants to serve, seeking guidance of personal purpose begins with the desire to connect with the 'greatest good' both within oneself and society" (pp. 180–181). In essence, the servant leader serves the community first so that the least privileged are the beneficiaries.

The servant leader who builds on the concept of developing a vision for the institution that grows out of the community culture has an excellent opportunity to serve effectively in a culture of trust. When followers recognize that the leader truly is a servant first and committed to the values of respect, service, and equity, the culture of trust comes naturally. No leader can be successful in an institution unless the followers truly trust the judgment and values of the leader. At the same time, the culture of trust is not a one-way street. The leader must trust the judgment and purpose of the followers. For example, the academic leader must understand the goals of the faculty and how each faculty member contributes to the attainment of those goals. With this knowledge, the academic leader can work with the faculty to develop strategies to attain these goals. Through such interaction, a level of trust evolves on both sides, and the leadership is more committed to the institution's culture.

Through the process of developing a curriculum and recruiting a faculty to carry out the mission of the college, the leader can lay the groundwork for a greater level of diversity in the faculty and administration. A commitment to servant leadership is critical, as there is sometimes a suspicion that the leader has a self-serving agenda that may not be consistent with faculty goals. If the leader is committed to carrying out the concept of servant leadership, the faculty will more readily recognize his or her dedication to promoting positive values that are not self-serving. The end result is a culture of trust.

The evolution of the culture of trust depends on viewing diversity not as an end in itself but as a goal that can be attained by the community. Success in meeting that goal is seen in the development of a learning community that demographically reflects society but philosophically builds on a foundation of the key values of respect, service, and equity leading to a mutual understanding of trust within the learning community. A culture of trust acknowledges that there are differences among cultures, and professionals can have differences of opinion relative to the way issues might be solved. However, a true culture of trust acknowledges these differences and seeks to learn from all cultures.

Conscious Development of Strategies

The fourth key to promoting diversity in academic leadership is a conscious development of the strategies to attain diversity. Throughout the history of higher education, many aggressive efforts have been made to promote diversity within organizations. In many states in the 1980s, universities and boards developed a "grow your own" program that encouraged minorities to pursue doctoral degrees in areas that had the greatest need. The results were mixed. However, the administrative staff at many universities did become more diverse by identifying minority staff or faculty members, sending them to school, and then hiring them in one of the institutions within the system.

Another way, perhaps more direct, to promote diversity in academic leadership is through aggressive recruitment of experienced people with strong academic qualifications. Search committees must recruit academically qualified individuals to positions of leadership to retain the trust of the faculty and maintain academic credibility, but at times it is essential to look beyond the obvious areas of scholarly preparation to see individuals who are well prepared in their discipline and committed to servant leadership. The most successful efforts occur when the chief academic officer and search committees consciously seek out individuals who break the barrier of race or gender and move them into leadership positions. This involves taking some risk, but if the person's core values are solid and he or she is committed to servant leadership, the risk is not nearly so great. Faculties and search committees must be willing to recognize the importance of administrative experience that is related to the academic mission while critically examining the commitment to scholarship. Members of the faculty are sometimes skeptical when there is no significant evidence of scholarly publications, but a strong administrator who is student oriented, sensitive to faculty, and committed to scholarly pursuits is very valuable. The search must be viewed as an opportunity to take a risk, go beyond the barriers erected by various constituents, and promote diversity in academic leadership by stepping outside the box. Identifying young minority faculty and providing limited administrative opportunities to them, while encouraging them to maintain a commitment to scholarship, will ultimately produce strong candidates for more challenging administrative opportunities. This can happen only if the faculty are willing to take such a risk.

Risk taking could be characterized as the fourth key to successful promotion of young faculty into leadership positions, but in reality it is not risky for the candidate if the senior administrator believes in the individual, is willing to stand by the individual, and at the same time continues to work with the faculty to gain a better understanding of the benefits of gender and ethnic diversity within that leadership role. This has occurred in many colleges, and ultimately these young leaders mature into outstanding department chairs or deans who subsequently move up in their profession. It is not enough to be committed to the moral goal or the organizational need; it is essential to be persistent and to be willing, when appropriate, to take risks.

One of the most discussed efforts to enhance diversity in academic leadership is affirmative action, which has been important to the success of moving minorities into leadership positions. Today it is being attacked, but it merits serious consideration within institutions and within systems and states. Contrary to what Selingo (2003) reports, diversity does benefit the institution. They write, "In a sense diversity is like free speech. Almost everyone approves of it in the abstract, but its application in concrete situations can produce great controversy" (p. 10). There is truth in that statement; however, if the diverse academic leadership in institutions has focused on core values and servant leadership, the likelihood of controversy is much less. In institutions that I have observed throughout the nation, diversity has not been a negative. It has been positive, and institutions have grown as a result. Students from different cultures living, studying, playing, and growing together learn from one another. If in this diverse community the values of respect, service, and equity are evident, the benefits will be great. Those benefits can best be seen in the campus culture.

Perhaps a better term than *affirmative action* would be *affirmative access,* because one of the strategies that can be used effectively in the promotion of diversity in academic leadership is an expansion of access at all levels to enhance the pool of opportunities that are available to individuals. Whether they are women, African Americans, Asians, Hispanics, Latinos, or others, there is little chance for service in the academic area unless there is a broadened base of access.

The success of affirmative action or affirmative access should not be measured just in terms of numbers of individuals promoted or hired into leadership positions; it also should be measured on the success of the individuals who serve the community. Obviously, numbers are important and cannot be ignored, but if significant numbers are employed and a high percentage are unsuccessful in providing leadership, the principles of affirmative action or affirmative access are undermined. Affirmative action, paired with the concept of servant leadership, can predictably lead to a higher level of success within communities. If those who are committed to the development of a culture of trust and a community of understanding recognize the nature of the constituency in which they serve, they will see that the results of the affirmative action efforts will be recognized as successful. In many instances, it is not the principle of affirmative action that is criticized but the results; therefore, if care is taken by the leadership team to build an understanding of servant leadership while affirmatively seeking minorities to be involved in that team, the response to the leadership will be more positive.

Willingness to Be Accountable

A final factor in the design of a program to promote diversity in academic leadership is to incorporate the concept of accountability. McGee-Cooper (1998) says,

> Why do we monitor rather than mentor people? Why does accountability end up last rather than first in our priorities? Why do we spend less time with those who we expect might "miss the mark" while giving those we expect to succeed our full attention? Is accountability as concerned with a person's

development as with what they produce? . . . If it [a system of accountability] is mutually created up front through the process of establishing servant leadership, a whole new paradigm emerges of what accountability means [p. 84].

The issue of accountability relates not only to the person serving, but also to whether the individuals being served are benefiting from this relationship. Look at those who are served, and see how they are developing. Mentor and encourage them as they develop leadership skills. Then establish some benchmarks to monitor the success of the students and the faculty who are served by the leader. Do the students continually have opportunities to enhance their academic experiences in and out of the classroom? Do members of the faculty have opportunities to continue to grow in their profession and become stronger teachers and stronger and more effective servants to students? Accountability that includes the concept of mentoring and focuses on appropriate outcomes is equally important to understanding the culture, the values, and the culture of trust to create diversity in leadership. The strategies used should focus not only on recruiting minorities into majority institutions but also on recruiting minority and majority leaders who understand and practice the principles of value-oriented servant leadership.

Conclusion

The challenge every college, university, and state higher education coordinating board has is changing demographics. In most states, minorities are becoming majorities, and the importance of gaining an understanding of other cultures becomes much more evident. To promote diversity in academic leadership, we must recognize that the college or university should be a microcosm of the total society, and in this setting we have the greatest opportunity to prepare community leaders to lead the new majorities. If we are successful, they will be modeling the servant leaders on our campuses. They will recognize the importance of a culture of trust and the commitment to service that is evident in servant leaders. Finally, they will use this community model as one that is applicable to the greater community. If we are unsuccessful, controversies will lead to unrest on campuses and in many communities. We must be persistent in focusing on visionary goals that transform and sustain the goals to attain diversity within the academic leadership of our institutions.

References

Bordas, J. "Power and Passion: Finding Personal Purpose." In L. Spears (ed.), *Reflections on Leadership*. New York: Wiley, 1995.

Covey, S. R. "The Mind-Set and Skill-Set of a Leader." In F. Hesselbein, M. Goldsmith, and I. Somerville (eds.), *Leading Beyond the Walls*. New York: Peter Drucker Foundation, 1999.

Diamond, R. M. (ed.). *Field Guide to Academic Leadership*. San Francisco: Jossey-Bass, 2002.

Ekman, R. "Standing Up When It Matters." *CIC Newsletter,* Apr. 2003, p. 2.

Greenleaf, R. *Servant as Leader*. Indianapolis: Robert K. Greenleaf Center for Servant Leadership, 1970.

McGee-Cooper, A. "Accountability as Covenant: The Tap Root of Servant Leadership." In L. C. Spears (ed.), *Insights on Leadership*. New York: Wiley, 1998.

Selingo, J. "New Study Questions Educational Benefits of Diversity." *Chronicle of Higher Education,* Mar. 28, 2003, p. A23.

Spears, L. C. (ed.). *Insights on Leadership*. New York: Wiley, 1998.

OSCAR C. PAGE *is president of Austin College in Sherman, Texas.*

9

Understanding the nature of academic leadership aids in the identification of both extrinsic and intrinsic rewards to motivate commitment to difficult yet critical roles in the academy.

The Rewards of Academic Leadership

Christina Murphy

Recent studies of academic leadership confirm what many academic leaders know from personal experience: academic leadership is a complex and demanding role with significant stress and high burnout and turnover rates (Brown, 2002; Brown and Moshavi, 2002). In the light of these issues, an exploration of the nature of academic leadership and its reward systems may provide significant insights into what factors motivate individuals to choose academic leadership roles and how these motivations and their outcomes might best be cultivated for the betterment of the leader and the academic institution he or she serves.

The Extrinsic and Intrinsic Rewards of Academic Leadership

Brown and Moshavi (2002), Rosenbach and Taylor (1993), Sontz (1991), and Kets de Vries and Zaleznik (1975) raise the question of what factors will draw individuals from one sphere in academics—usually the sphere of teaching and scholarship—into the sphere of administration. One answer may lie in organizational commitment, which generally is defined as an exchange in which an individual becomes psychologically attached to an organization in return for the gains or benefits provided by the organization (Angle, 1983; Angle and Perry, 1981). Young, Worchel, and Woehr (1998) contend that organizational commitment is one of the most important factors that motivate individuals to choose leadership roles.

In several studies, researchers have found support for a connection between organizational commitment and intrinsic and extrinsic rewards (Flynn and Solomon, 1985; Caldwell, Chatman, and O'Reilly, 1980).

Generally, extrinsic rewards are viewed as the benefits organizations provide to individuals who are successful in fulfilling social roles, while intrinsic rewards are the personal satisfactions individuals achieve in carrying out the duties and responsibilities of those roles (Hackman and Oldham, 1976). Interestingly, when investigators seek to determine the relative importance of extrinsic and intrinsic rewards as predictors for organizational commitment, the majority of research findings suggest that organizational commitment is more strongly associated with intrinsic rewards than extrinsic rewards (O'Reilly and Caldwell, 1980).

In academics, extrinsic rewards for leadership roles are many: social and professional status, higher salaries, career mobility and advancement, greater institutional authority, and professional recognition, to name but a few. The intrinsic rewards often are less immediately visible but also still strongly influence both personal motivations and professional career choices. Intrinsic rewards relate to a desire for personal satisfaction with one's actions and achievements, and theorists generally see a connection between intrinsic satisfaction and the individual's psychological makeup. For example, Torrance (1976) claims that individuals receive "very rich intrinsic rewards" from the exercise of their talents (p. 146), and Maxwell (2003) views the development of character as an intrinsic reward for leadership skills that are conducted in a spirit that respects the views of all involved.

Adding to the complexity of extrinsic and intrinsic rewards is the fact that most individuals in academic leadership roles tend to be midcareer professionals who typically have reached the peak performance period of their careers, thus benefiting from years of professional and personal development (Slocum and Cron, 1985). London (1983) suggests that the decisions and actions of midcareer professionals relate to career identity, career insight, and career resilience and that these aspects overlap with the human needs of affiliation, esteem, and self-actualization. Maslow (1970) posits a similar view in asserting that motivation can be based on a hierarchy of human needs, the highest of which is self-actualization. Berkowitz, Fraser, Treasure, and Cochran (1987) find that a significant reason intrinsic rewards are so important to midcareer professionals is that career-oriented professionals view work as part of a lifetime plan, a plan to be monitored and nurtured so that they may achieve professional and personal goals. Thus, job structure and personal recognition often are more important to career professionals than pay because the monetary significance of pay is secondary to the organizational recognition it provides. Similarly, a number of studies have found that career-oriented individuals, especially those at midcareer, often desire to apply and further develop professional skills to achieve or to enhance their peak performance (Romzek, 1989; Shaffer, 1987; Korman, Wittig-Berman, and Lang, 1981). In essence, these professionals are following the arc of self-actualization that Maslow (1970) and London (1983) describe as a motivational behavior with broad implications for personal growth.

Intrinsic Rewards and Personal Enrichment

The emphasis on the personal qualities of the leader noted by these researchers raises the question of whether the intrinsic personal qualities required of an effective leader can also be aspects of an intrinsic reward system. Champy and Nohria (2000) attribute nearly all such intrinsic motivations to ambition, which they define as "the spirit of success, of striving for something worth achieving" (p. 1). As they note, for highly motivated individuals who exemplify the drive toward self-actualization, the intrinsic rewards of leadership are many. A leadership role can fulfill the person's ambition and desire to excel. Leaders who are called on to define and accomplish the major goals of their units or universities generally find personal fulfillment in thinking creatively to solve problems and initiate new actions. Often such individuals speak of the rewards of academic leadership in terms of shaping a future or leaving a legacy—in essence, in terms of making a difference. Such high levels of accomplishment provide significant intrinsic rewards, especially in terms of the attainment of one's ego ideal or ideal image of self, which, Freud (1990) contends, often directs a person's life choices toward the fulfillment of significant goals.

Leadership and Shared Experiences

Among the intrinsic rewards of academic leadership is the fact that it is rooted in the principles and value structures of shared experiences, which help to define both identity and purpose in human existence (Taylor, 1989). Erikson (1974, 1977) has elaborated a general theory of organizational development around concepts of the generative processes in shared experiences: (1) the shared values and visions by which people recognize an institution or organization and come together as members in a common mission and (2) the practical judgments, roles, and rules by which participants keep their action in line with the mission.

To lead the members of a group and structure their participation toward the achievement of significant institutional goals, the leader must create a sense of shared experiences to form the core of the bond that he or she and the group members forge to move from vision or concept to action and goal. Interestingly, many academic leaders come from the ranks of classroom teachers. Teaching is another interpersonal transaction that involves shared experiences—in this case, between the professor and the students. Those who progress into leadership roles may hesitate in leaving teaching behind as their primary work because they fear they will miss that level of shared experience and bonding that occurred with their students. The discovery that the significance of shared experiences continues in the leadership role, though with different contours and impacts, is often a pleasant and satisfying realization that enriches the leadership experience for many academics.

Certainly, this aspect of shared experiences is a valued component of the mentoring that many leaders will do for those who are beginning their journeys into leadership roles and will benefit strongly from interactions with an experienced leader who serves as a mentor and role model in this learning process. Above all, shared experiences tend to be libratory in nature by providing settings and structures in which the personal qualities and talents of the leader can emerge. Often the "higher good" that academics speak of in the work of the institution as a public trust for the betterment of society finds its roots in the libratory dimensions of shared experiences that can draw the best from people in the type of altruistic thinking that goes beyond self and toward the greater good of the whole (Nissim and Robutti, 1992).

Romer and Whipple (1991) contend that this mode of thinking makes collaborating "across the power line" of leadership and authority possible and also constitutes an especially effective form of education (p. 66). In this regard, leadership skills represent a dynamic integration of management or organizational skills and interpersonal abilities. Romer and Whipple (1991) state that this nexus represents a "transition from cooperation to collaboration" that occurs when the authority in a given situation is redefined by an "abrupt cognitive shift" in which the leader begins to construct his or her own knowledge and recognizes his or her own authority in the process (p. 68). Ultimately, this new realization of personal growth as a leader becomes "learnedness: the combination of knowledge acquired and experience expressed" (p. 66). As Romer and Whipple state, "Indeed, the word *authority* has the same root as *author,* and both may be traced back ultimately to the Latin root *augere,* meaning to augment or to induce growth" (p. 68).

Many researchers view mentoring as a unique shared experience and also one of the most significant rewards of academic leadership. The mentor-protégé relationship is a special type of shared experience that goes beyond merely advising and guiding others; it also involves behaving in ways that indicate respect for protégés as sources of ideas and insights. In this view, mentoring is a transformative relationship in which the mentor is actively invested in shaping the protégé's worldview and in developing the protégé's talents and contributions to the institution and to society. In return, the mentor's rewards lie in potential career enhancement, the development of an information network, access to the protégé as a trusted adviser, and the personal satisfaction of helping someone (Zey, 1984). Together, the mentor and protégé earn respect for their joint accomplishments and for their efficiency and dedication as a team. Furthermore, the mentor experiences the psychological rewards of pride in the protégé's accomplishments and the personal satisfaction involved in contributing to the institution's overall success (Zey, 1984).

Conclusion

Certainly, the numerous research studies on leadership reach similar conclusions on the satisfactions to be drawn from leadership roles. In the broadest sense, leadership provides the intrinsic reward of creating new structures—a process that brings ideas from the realm of the speculative into the world of the actual. Invariably, there are positive psychological rewards to be derived from such higher-level accomplishments. In the Freudian schema, the ego ideal is reached, in which a highly competent and highly motivated individual affirms his or her competency and receives the rewards of recognition, appreciation, and professional advancement.

The shared experiences of collaboration also provide a rich source of reward for leaders. Fairholm (1994) has examined the relationship of leaders with those they lead and asserts that "leadership is not so much what individual leaders do as it is what leader and led do collectively. . . . [because] leadership is not so much a function of the individual leader as it is a condition of the culture. While leadership may be spontaneous at times, most often it is a result of specific, planned actions by individual leaders to create organizational cultures characterized by internal harmony around values and ideals the leader and follower share or come to share" (p. 7).

This capacity to create "organizational cultures characterized by internal harmony" emerges from both motivation and volition, with knowledge as the mediating force (Royce, 1961). Deal and Kennedy (2000) support this view and argue that the knowledge of an institution's culture is what enables the leader to implement the "core values" (p. 24) that create unity and purpose and ultimately translate into visionary thinking on the leader's part.

In considering the value of academic leadership, extrinsic and intrinsic rewards are always at play. Status, authority, and institutional power form the core of extrinsic rewards, but equally as valuable to the leader— perhaps even more so—are the intrinsic aspects of personal growth, cognitive realizations, and the shared experiences of collaboration and mentoring. In this regard, Tierney (1989) is correct in asserting that "transformative leadership is centrally concerned with developing and maintaining the common values of an institution" and that "transformative leaders must have an intimate involvement with the life of the institution" (p. 160). Luke (1986) defines this perspective as the dynamics of interdependence and interconnectedness, which are brought about by the catalytic leadership skills of public administrators who understand new ways of conceptualizing their roles in the interconnected world of contemporary society. Bailey (1992) calls this ability and its outcomes a "multiversalist paradigm" (p. 34) in which expertise combines with personhood to achieve far greater results than what would be achieved through expertise alone.

Ultimately, using one's talents toward positive aims and receiving recognition in the process are significant rewards of academic leadership. Gorostiaga (1999) claims that the development of human potential is the most important function of academic institutions and, by extension, of the academic leaders who shape those institutions and position them to respond to new social demands and challenges. Thus, academic institutions of the twenty-first century require leaders who appreciate the enormous value to be found in bringing order to institutions through an admixture of leadership qualities and organizational and societal priorities.

Successfully achieving each aspect of this mutually dependent process for the betterment of the institution and the people and social systems it serves may well prove to be the most significant reward of academic leadership.

References

Angle, H. "Organizational Commitment: Individual and Organizational Influences." *Sociology of Work and Occupations,* 1983, *10,* 123–146.

Angle, H., and Perry, J. "An Empirical Assessment of Organizational Commitment and Organizational Effectiveness." *Administrative Science Quarterly,* 1981, *26,* 1–14.

Bailey, M. T. "Beyond Rationality: Decision-Making in an Interconnected World." In M. T. Bailey and R. T. Mayer (eds.), *Public Management in an Interconnected World: Essays in the Minnowbrook Tradition.* Westport, Conn.: Greenwood Press, 1992.

Berkowitz, L., Fraser, C., Treasure, F. P., and Cochran, S. "Pay, Equity, Job Gratifications, and Comparisons in Pay Satisfaction." *Journal of Applied Psychology,* 1987, *72*(4), 544–551.

Brown, F. W. "Inspiration, More Than Rewards, Improves Faculty Effectiveness." *Academic Leader,* 2002, *18*(9), 1, 8.

Brown, F. W., and Moshavi, D. "Herding Academic Cats: Faculty Reactions to Transformational and Contingent Reward Leadership by Department Chairs." *Journal of Leadership Studies,* 2002, *8*(3), 79–93.

Caldwell, D. F., Chatman, J. A., and O'Reilly, C. A. "Building Organizational Commitment: A Multifirm Study." *Journal of Occupational Psychology,* 1990, *63,* 245–261.

Champy, J. A., and Nohria, N. *The Arc of Ambition: Defining the Leadership Journey.* Cambridge, Mass.: Perseus Books, 2000.

Deal, T. E., and Kennedy, A. A. *Corporate Cultures: The Rites and Rituals of Corporate Life.* Cambridge, Mass.: Perseus Books, 2000.

Erikson, E. H. *Dimensions of a New Identity: The Jefferson Lectures of 1973.* New York: Morrow, 1974.

Erikson, E. H. *Toys and Reasons: The Godkin Lectures of 1972.* New York: Morrow, 1977.

Fairholm, G. W. *Leadership and the Culture of Trust.* Westport, Conn.: Praeger, 1994.

Flynn, D. M., and Solomon, E. "Organizational Commitment: A Multivariate Test Within the Banking Industry." *Psychological Reports,* 1985, *57,* 124–129.

Freud, S. *The Ego and the Id* (J. Riviere, trans.). New York: Norton, 1990. (Originally published 1923.)

Gorostiaga, X.S.J. "In Search of the Missing Link Between Education and Development." In P. G. Altbach (ed.), *Private Prometheus: Private Higher Education and Development in the Twenty-First Century.* Westport, Conn.: Greenwood Press, 1999.

Hackman, R., and Oldham, G. R. "Motivation Through the Design of Work: Test of a Theory." *Organizational Behavior and Human Performance,* 1976, *16,* 250–279.

Kets de Vries, M.F.R., and Zaleznik, A. *Power and the Corporate Mind.* Boston: Houghton Mifflin, 1975.

Korman, A. K., Wittig-Berman, U., and Lang, D. "Career Success and Personal Failure: Alienation in Professionals and Managers." *Academy of Management Journal,* 1981, *24*(2), 342–360.

London, M. "Toward a Theory of Career Motivation." *Academy of Management Review,* 1983, *8*(4), 620–630.

Luke, J. S. "Managing Interconnectedness: The Need for Catalytic Leadership." *Futures Research Quarterly,* 1986, *2,* 73–84.

Maslow, A. *Motivation and Personality.* New York: HarperCollins, 1970.

Maxwell, J. C. *The Twenty-One Indispensable Qualities of a Leader: Becoming the Person Others Will Want to Follow.* New York: Thomas Nelson, 2003.

Nissim, L. M., and Robutti, A. *Shared Experience: The Psychoanalytic Dialogue*. London: Karnac Books, 1992.

O'Reilly, C. A., and Caldwell, D. F. "Job Choice: The Impact of Intrinsic and Extrinsic Factors on Subsequent Satisfaction and Commitment." *Journal of Applied Psychology*, 1980, *65*, 559–565.

Romer, K. T., and Whipple, W. R. "Collaboration Across the Power Line." *College Teaching*, 1991, *39*(2), 66–71.

Romzek, B. S. "Personal Consequences of Employee Commitment." *Academy of Management Journal*, 1989, *32*(3), 649–661.

Rosenbach, W., and Taylor, R. *Contemporary Issues in Leadership*. Boulder, Colo.: Westview Press, 1993.

Royce, J. E. *Man and His Nature: A Philosophical Psychology*. New York: McGraw-Hill, 1961.

Shaffer, G. S. "Patterns of Work and Nonwork Satisfaction." *Journal of Applied Psychology*, 1987, *72*(1), 115–124.

Slocum, J. W., Jr., and Cron, W. L. "Job Attitude and Performance During Three Career Stages." *Journal of Vocational Behavior*, 1985, *26*(2), 126–145.

Sontz, A.H.L. *The American College President, 1636–1989: A Critical Review and Bibliography*. Westport, Conn.: Greenwood Press, 1991.

Taylor C. *Sources of the Self: The Making of Modern Identity*. Cambridge, Mass.: Harvard University Press, 1989.

Tierney, W. G. *Curricular Landscapes, Democratic Vistas: Transformative Leadership in Higher Education*. Westport, Conn.: Praeger, 1989.

Torrance, E. P. *Guiding Creative Talent*. Huntington, N.Y.: R. E. Krieger, 1976.

Tuckman, B. W., and Johnson, F. C. *Effective College Management: The Outcome Approach*. Westport, Conn.: Greenwood Press, 1987.

Young, B. S., Worchel, S., and Woehr, D. J. "Organizational Commitment Among Public Service Employees." *Public Personnel Management*, 1998, *27*(3), 339–348.

Zey, M. G. *The Mentor Connection*. Homewood, Ill.: Dow Jones–Irwin, 1984.

CHRISTINA MURPHY *is dean of the College of Liberal Arts and professor of English at Marshall University in Huntington, West Virginia.*

10

Bedside manner is about relationships, and tailoring attitudes, approaches, and demeanor to accommodate individuals results in improved collegiality.

Bedside Manner and Effective Academic Administrative Leadership

Daryl Gilley

It was late on a Thursday afternoon when I walked into the dean's office for what I thought would be a rather pedestrian conversation about a new model for the summer term class schedule. Dr. Ivey was at his desk, head in his hands, an almost perceptible cloud of despair hovering over him. "Bob, what in the world is the matter?" I asked. His response, more of a statement than an answer, went something like this.

"You know," he said, "I'm a fairly optimistic, upbeat kind of guy. During the past year, I've been working hard and making some success toward creating a great academic team, or so I thought. I've been spending long days and weekends making plans, expecting results, holding meetings, creating new initiatives, assuming that everyone is on the same page, playing the same song, on the same team. You know all the clichés. Evidently I've been totally clueless about the real state of affairs in this department. It seems that every new initiative runs into some insurmountable obstacle. Important details are overlooked. People's feelings get hurt but you don't know it for weeks, and blame is being cast about like confetti in the wind. For the longest time, I couldn't figure it out, but now I understand. I'll tell you what I think. I think there are forces of evil at work here. They do their work behind closed office doors. They lurk in the dark hallways and conspire in the lounges. They refer to themselves as colleagues, but that's only a pseudonym; they haven't shown their true colors. They've been patiently waiting, baiting me with the possibility of cooperation and collegiality. But now I know. They're incapable of trust and cooperation. These . . ."

NEW DIRECTIONS FOR HIGHER EDUCATION, no. 124, Winter 2003 © Wiley Periodicals, Inc.

"Wait," I said, breaking into his tragic monologue. I suggested that surely he was just having a bad day, that things could not be that bad.

"Oh yes they are," he declared. "I don't know whether their behavior is genetic or an effect of the environment, but it's real. And they can't change, or won't change. I'm certain of it. They tease me with the appearance of trust and cooperation. We discuss issues until we're exhausted, but it is too great a challenge for them. I have learned their true nature. They are incapable of understanding the big picture. They seem to listen, but they don't hear.

"You know," he continued, "it's overwhelming; it's frustrating; and it's demoralizing. It is destroying my spirit! It simply isn't worth the effort. The grandest of our dreams, the most noble of our causes, has become a mere afterthought. The failure wasn't due to any groundswell of resistance but by an inability to be convinced. I give up. They have won simply by their ability to resist change by doing nothing."

If you have ever been anywhere near this place in your life, I am sure you will agree it is a lonely and desolate land with seemingly insurmountable obstacles. Living in a place even remotely like this may prove to be a terminal condition, recovery almost impossible. So the secret is to avoid this place. If you take a wrong turn, ask directions immediately, back up, and get back on the right road.

In this chapter, I address one small aspect of the leadership algorithm: communication. As the title of this chapter suggests, the aspect of communication we will be dealing with is that nebulous part of the human interaction process that sets the stage—the one that results in creative problem solving and collegial relationships.

So this chapter is about the interpersonal aspects of communication. But it is so much more than bedside manner, which can be superficial and suited to the moment, as in an emotion feigned. Bedside manner as understood here is about relationships—how they are built, how they are maintained, and how they are mended. It is where minds, souls, and hearts form connections. It is the precursor that lays the groundwork for the interactions we have with each other in our daily work lives. It is about how we can make each and every one of those interactions a quality moment that reaffirms trust in the organization and in our decision to be a part of it.

In addressing this topic, I rely on over thirty years of personal experience in higher education. During that time, I have made more mistakes than I care to remember. Nevertheless, I have learned a few things about working with people. I do not consider myself an expert on human relationships by any stretch of the imagination, so reader beware: take what is presented as what it is—an observation and recollection of life in the academy from the perspective of both a member of the faculty and an administrator. I am not going to suggest anything you do not already know. Knowing is not the hard part. The hard part is having the courage to act on our better instincts when that is personally painful because it threatens our self-esteem or our position. The hard part is being man or woman enough to admit we are wrong, and publicly if need be. The hard part is facing difficult situations with courage and conviction. The hard part is acting on principle when politics rears its ugly head. The hard part is treating others with respect, trust, dignity, and concern, even when they do not deserve it.

The tools required to be an effective academic administrative leader are not present at birth. Most of us are gifted, possessing strengths in one area or another, and nearly all of us have learned to survive, if not thrive, in our respective roles. Few of us, however, possess the entire catalogue of leadership traits that the experts suggest exemplary leaders should have. Some of us are more charismatic, some more scholarly, and some better fiscal managers. Individuals who have studied effective leaders have suggested numerous characteristics they hold in common: honesty, vision, competence, charisma, intelligence, courage., and many others. We will look at some practical applications of bedside manner, but before we do, consider this assumption:

Assumption: Bedside manner consists of a combination of attitude, approach, and demeanor.

Attitude: It may be hard at times, but assume that everyone in the organization wants to do a good job. Not one person in the department, division, or college arrives at work in the morning with the intent of undermining, demoralizing, or tearing down.

Approach: To approach someone always heightens his or her innate fear of the unknown. If you are a supervisor, this effect is even more dramatic when you approach a person you supervise.

Demeanor: Appearance, outward manner, and nonverbal cues communicate more than anything you say. The way we appear to others is almost always different from the way we think we appear.

Practical applications: Or who are these people and how do I work with them?

What follows are some professional types we have all encountered and a few suggested approaches to dealing with them. Table 10.1 presents a summary of these types.

The Neophyte

The neophyte can be a joy to work with: bright-eyed, innocent, easily led, typically energetic and idealistic. The easily led aspect of the neophyte's makeup is problematic. For the neophyte, the most important aspect of the environment is the relationship developed with other faculty or staff. Providing the neophyte with a compatible mentor can go a long way toward ensuring that he is not led astray by incorrect, incomplete, biased, or prejudiced opinions.

**Table 10.1. Professional Types and Interactive Strategies:
A Summary**

Type	Strategy
The Neophyte	Provide a mentor
The Loner	Bring into the fold
The Idealist	Listen and compliment
The Team Player	Reward
The Subversive	Confront
The Shopworn	Encourage and recognize
The Journeyman	Ensure quality tools of the trade
The Star	Provide outlets for expression
The Obstructionist	Remove the base of influence
The Cynic	Listen
The Sage	Listen and question
The Incompetent	Remediate or terminate
The Lazy	Require productivity

Bedside Strategy: Seek out the neophyte on a regular basis. Make opportunities to mentor. Develop a relationship. The neophyte will evolve into an asset or a liability. Make sure it is an asset.

The Loner

A person may be considered a loner for any number of reasons. It has been my experience that even the most curmudgeonly among us have more fulfilling lives and realize greater productivity working together than in isolation. Loners should be brought into the fold when opportunity presents itself. Their condition is not a disease, so they should not be shunned, punished, or embarrassed. Rather, they should be purposely included on committees, lunch groups, and impromptu conversations. They may have something significant to contribute but just have not been asked. Whether socially inept or a loner by choice, the educational process is driven by people and, at its best, by people working together.

Bedside Strategy: Unlike the neophyte, the loner has chosen a lifestyle. Get to know her. If she would rather be included, make sure that it happens. If she would rather be a lone ranger, encourage her to participate so that others can benefit from her knowledge.

The Idealist

The idealist is our conscience. Listen to him. Take care not to dismiss his contribution as naive. The idealist can be a thorn in the flesh because he demands that we examine our motives and our priorities. If, as we have been taught, the unexamined life is not worth living, then perhaps the unexamined motive is not worth pursuing.

Bedside Strategy: Make sure to speak regularly to the idealist. We all need to occasionally have our dreams rekindled, our compass recalibrated.

The Team Player

Thank goodness for the team player who is always ready to serve. She participates in discussions, feels free to disagree, and can eagerly work toward a goal that is not particularly interesting to her because it is in the interest of the organization to do so. The team player may be one of the most important resources an organization has. We can easily take the team player for granted because we desire and expect her behavior. The team player should not be confused with a "yes man." Through private and public recognition of specific activities of the best team players, perhaps we can recruit more players to the team, which is really what we want.

Bedside Strategy: Be careful not to take her for granted. Make sure the team player feels appreciated. Recognize this person publicly whenever appropriate.

The Subversive

If the team player is a blessing, the subversive is a curse. He must be reclaimed or removed. Reclamation is always better, if at all possible. I think the only way to deal with this type is straight on. As a subversive, he is uncomfortable with straightforward interaction. Avoid pointing fingers or laying blame. Deal with the facts. Ask yourself why the individual pursues subversive tactics. Ask the individual why he acts in the way that he does. Many times the precipitating issue or cause can be remedied, and the subversive can become an ally. The subversive may have rationalized his actions as being heroic or "quixotic," a fight for good in an evil empire. If this is the case, you have some one-on-one work to do, but there is hope. If the subversive is acting without legitimate reason, as retribution for past grievances, real or imagined, the cause is probably lost.

Bedside Strategy: Although we wish he would just go away, he probably will not. The subversive needs to be engaged. Make sure you know the facts. Share enough information with him to ensure that he knows you have the facts, but avoid accusation unless you are willing to go to the wall. Remember that your goal is to reclaim the subversive, to rechannel his destructive energy. A weak or poorly informed leader will rarely be successful with the subversive.

The Shopworn

Life eventually makes us shopworn, so we all need encouragement and recognition. This is especially true of the individual who for years has been toiling daily, doing a good job, seeking neither fame nor fortune, but taking solace from a job well done. Whether in the classroom, the office suite, or on the grounds with the maintenance crew, this person needs to be recognized. Human beings need to feel that what they do—what they have invested their lives in—is deemed worthy by others. Consider something as simple as a comment such as, "I heard about your work on the Academic Affairs Committee. Keep up the good work. Is there anything we can do to help you do your job better? I appreciate what you do." A note to express appreciation for exceptional effort can give recognition and encouragement. It is so little to give.

Bedside Strategy: Find a way to refresh her spirit. That means finding out what is important to her and creating an opportunity or allowing her to work in that arena.

The Journeyman

The journeyman is similar to the shopworn, but perhaps a little less haggard. The journeyman also takes pride in his craft. He is a person who uses and appreciates good tools. Provide the journeyman with the quality tools of his trade. His productivity will increase, and he will love working at his job even more than he already does.

Bedside Strategy: Find a way to recognize his work personally and publicly. Ask questions about how the work was accomplished. The divine is in the details for someone who loves his work.

The Star

A few of us are fortunate to work with extraordinary professionals such as the director of library services who through sheer force of will can make the ordinary outstanding, the English teacher who can bring poetry to life, the developmental math teacher who can explain why we really need algebra, the dean who can motivate a group of faculty to accomplish so much more than they could on their own. The extraordinary need avenues for expression. The interesting thing about the extraordinary is that more of them are around than you might at first realize. Seek them out. Give them a chance. So what if they turn out to only be ordinary? You will be extraordinary in their eyes.

Bedside Strategy: Stars deserve star status. Find out what motivates the star performer and ensure that the need is met, or she will find another venue for her creative talents.

The Obstructionist

Occasionally there are people whose actions can be counted on to impede progress. They are against everything, firmly rooted to some distant past that never existed. These people must be turned. If they cannot be turned, then they must be removed from any sphere of influence.

Bedside Strategy: Once absolutely certain of the fact that the person is an obstructionist, confront him with the facts. Ask for an explanation. Perhaps there is a good one; if so, be prepared to respond.

The Cynic

Some types are more enjoyable to deal with than others. The cynic can wear you down, and it is easy to brush her off with little or no consideration, hoping that she, like the subversive, will go away. She will not, so find out why she is so cynical. Perhaps it is for good reason. Even though it is painful, hear her out. She may have reason to be cynical, and that reason may need to be dealt with.

Bedside Strategy: Force yourself to talk with the cynic on occasion. Hear her out. But be prepared to live with this type. Some people just love to be miserable.

The Sage

The sage is much more interesting to talk with than the cynic. Usually experienced and pragmatic, the sage may speak little but say much. It is important to hear him out, to ask probing questions to extract from him the truths that he may or may not share easily. The sage may wax philosophical and speak in what seems to be riddles, but listening will be worth the effort.

Bedside Strategy: Have lunch with the sage. Bounce ideas off him. Listen carefully to what he has to say. Allow time to explore ideas deeply.

The Incompetent

Unfortunately, some people find themselves in a job for which they are totally ill prepared and have chosen to remain in the job, as uncomfortable as it must be. A situation such as this cannot continue. It is a disservice to the people we are attempting to serve and an embarrassment to the institution. No self-respecting supervisor will, on discovery of this situation, allow it to continue.

Three solutions present themselves: terminate the individual in question, provide corrective training if appropriate, or reassign the individual to a position where her strengths can be better used. To do nothing is not an option.

Bedside Strategy: The incompetent never realizes that she may be the problem. You will not convince her. Deal with the problem.

The Lazy

As hard as it is to believe for most of us, some people are just lazy. Considering the effort it takes to avoid work, though, I wonder if they are truly lazy or if something else more sinister is taking place. The lazy must be productive just like the rest of us. For these people, productivity goals that can be tracked may help the situation. Typically the requirement that the person be productive either corrects the problem or the problem goes away on its own.

Bedside Strategy: Deal with the lazy as with the incompetent, but with less sympathy.

Conclusion

Effective communication is more than just sending and receiving a message. Communication will be at its most effective only when it is the by-product of relationships that are built on mutual trust and respect. These relationships are built one at a time, one person at a time.

Communication, being a most human attribute, is also fraught with all other things most human: distrust, fear, turf protection, petty politics, and so on. The ability to communicate effectively is not as common as one might expect, but it is essential to effective leadership.

DARYL GILLEY *is president of West Georgia Technical College in LaGrange, Georgia.*

INDEX

Back Issue/Subscription Order Form

Copy or detach and send to:

Jossey-Bass, A Wiley Company, 989 Market Street, San Francisco CA 94103-1741

Call or fax toll-free: Phone 888-378-2537 6:30AM – 3PM PST; Fax 888-481-2665

Back Issues: Please send me the following issues at $29 each
(Important: please include series initials and issue number, such as HE114.)

_____

_____

_____

$ _____ Total for single issues

$ _____ SHIPPING CHARGES: SURFACE   Domestic   Canadian

	Domestic	Canadian
First Item	$5.00	$6.00
Each Add'l Item	$3.00	$1.50

For next-day and second-day delivery rates, call the number listed above.

Subscriptions: Please __start __renew my subscription to *New Directions for Higher Education* for the year 2____at the following rate:

U.S.	__Individual $80	__Institutional $160
Canada	__Individual $80	__Institutional $200
All Others	__Individual $104	__Institutional $234
Online Subscription		__Institutional $176

**For more information about online subscriptions visit
www.interscience.wiley.com**

$ _____ Total single issues and subscriptions (Add appropriate sales tax for your state for single issue orders. No sales tax for U.S. subscriptions. Canadian residents, add GST for subscriptions and single issues.)

__Payment enclosed (U.S. check or money order only)

__VISA __MC __AmEx # _____ Exp. Date _____

Signature _____ Day Phone _____

__ Bill Me (U.S. institutional orders only. Purchase order required.)

Purchase order # _____

Federal Tax ID13559302   **GST 89102 8052**

Name _____

Address _____

_____

Phone _____ E-mail _____

For more information about Jossey-Bass, visit our Web site at www.josseybass.com

**NEW DIRECTIONS FOR HIGHER EDUCATION
IS NOW AVAILABLE ONLINE AT WILEY INTERSCIENCE**

What is Wiley InterScience?

Wiley InterScience is the dynamic online content service from John Wiley &
Sons delivering the full text of over 300 leading scientific, technical, medical,
and professional journals, plus major reference works, the acclaimed *Current
Protocols* laboratory manuals, and even the full text of select Wiley print books
online.

What are some special features of Wiley InterScience?

Wiley InterScience Alerts is a service that delivers table of contents via e-mail
for any journal available on Wiley InterScience as soon as a new issue is
published online.
Early View is Wiley's exclusive service presenting individual articles online as
soon as they are ready, even before the release of the compiled print issue.
These articles are complete, peer-reviewed, and citable.
CrossRef is the innovative multi-publisher reference linking system enabling
readers to move seamlessly from a reference in a journal article to the cited
publication, typically located on a different server and published by a different
publisher.

How can I access Wiley InterScience?

Visit http://www.interscience.wiley.com

Guest Users can browse Wiley InterScience for unrestricted access to journal
Tables of Contents and Article Abstracts, or use the powerful search engine.
Registered Users are provided with a *Personal Home Page* to store and
manage customized alerts, searches, and links to favorite journals and articles.
Additionally, Registered Users can view free Online Sample Issues and preview
selected material from major reference works.
Licensed Customers are entitled to access full-text journal articles in PDF, with
select journals also offering full-text HTML.

How do I become an Authorized User?

Authorized Users are individuals authorized by a paying Customer to have
access to the journals in Wiley InterScience. For example, a university that
subscribes to Wiley journals is considered to be the Customer. Faculty, staff and
students authorized by the university to have access to those journals in Wiley
InterScience are Authorized Users. Users should contact their Library for information on which Wiley journals they have access to in Wiley InterScience.

ASK YOUR INSTITUTION ABOUT WILEY INTERSCIENCE TODAY!

United States Postal Service
Statement of Ownership, Management, and Circulation

1. Publication Title	2. Publication Number	3. Filing Date
New Directions For Higher Education	0 2 7 1 - 0 5 6 0	9/30/03

4. Issue Frequency	5. Number of Issues Published Annually	6. Annual Subscription Price
Quarterly	4	$80 Individual $160 Institution

7. Complete Mailing Address of Known Office of Publication (Not printer) (Street, city, county, state, and ZIP+4)

989 Market Street
San Francisco, CA 94103-1741
San Francisco County

Contact Person: Joe Schuman
Telephone: 415 782 3232

8. Complete Mailing Address of Headquarters or General Business Office of Publisher (Not printer)

Same as above

9. Full Names and Complete Mailing Addresses of Publisher, Editor, and Managing Editor (Do not leave blank)

Publisher (Name and complete mailing address)

Wiley, San Francisco
Jossey-Bass Pfeiffer
Address - same as above

Editor (Name and complete mailing address)

Martin Kramer
2807 Shasta Road
Berkeley, CA 94708

Managing Editor (Name and complete mailing address)

None

10. Owner (Do not leave blank. If the publication is owned by a corporation, give the name and address of the corporation immediately followed by the names and addresses of all stockholders owning or holding 1 percent or more of the total amount of stock. If not owned by a corporation, give the names and addresses of the individual owners. If owned by a partnership or other unincorporated firm, give its name and address as well as those of each individual owner. If the publication is published by a nonprofit organization, give its name and address.)

Full Name	Complete Mailing Address
John Wiley & Sons Inc.	111 River Street Hoboken, NJ 07030
Same as above	Same as above

11. Known Bondholders, Mortgagees, and Other Security Holders Owning or Holding 1 Percent or More of Total Amount of Bonds, Mortgages, or Other Securities. If none, check box. ▶ ☐ None

Full Name	Complete Mailing Address

12. Tax Status (For completion by nonprofit organizations authorized to mail at nonprofit rates) (Check one)
The purpose, function, and nonprofit status of this organization and the exempt status for federal income tax purposes:
☐ Has Not Changed During Preceding 12 Months
☐ Has Changed During Preceding 12 Months (Publisher must submit explanation of change with this statement)

PS Form 3526, October 1999 (See Instructions on Reverse)

13. Publication Title	14. Issue Date for Circulation Data Below
New Directions For Higher Education	Summer 2003

15.	Extent and Nature of Circulation	Average No. Copies Each Issue During Preceding 12 Months	No. Copies of Single Issue Published Nearest to Filing Date
a.	Total Number of Copies (Net press run)	1,627	1,596
b. Paid and/or Requested Circulation	(1) Paid/Requested Outside-County Mail Subscriptions Stated on Form 3541. (Include advertiser's proof and exchange copies)	901	928
	(2) Paid In-County Subscriptions Stated on Form 3541 (Include advertiser's proof and exchange copies)	0	0
	(3) Sales Through Dealers and Carriers, Street Vendors, Counter Sales, and Other Non-USPS Paid Distribution	0	0
	(4) Other Classes Mailed Through the USPS	0	0
c.	Total Paid and/or Requested Circulation (Sum of 15b. (1), (2),(3),and (4)) ▶	901	928
d. Free Distribution by Mail (Samples, complimentary, and other free)	(1) Outside-County as Stated on Form 3541	0	0
	(2) In-County as Stated on Form 3541	0	0
	(3) Other Classes Mailed Through the USPS	1	1
e.	Free Distribution Outside the Mail (Carriers or other means)	87	88
f.	Total Free Distribution (Sum of 15d. and 15e.) ▶	88	89
g.	Total Distribution (Sum of 15c. and 15f.) ▶	989	1,017
h.	Copies not Distributed	638	579
i.	Total (Sum of 15g. and h.) ▶	1,627	1,596
j.	Percent Paid and/or Requested Circulation (15c. divided by 15g. times 100)	91%	91%

16. Publication of Statement of Ownership
☐ Publication required. Will be printed in the Winter 2003 issue of this publication. ☐ Publication not required.

17. Signature and Title of Editor, Publisher, Business Manager, or Owner — Susan E. Lewis VP & Publisher – Periodicals — Date 9/30/03

I certify that all information furnished on this form is true and complete. I understand that anyone who furnishes false or misleading information on this form or who omits material or information requested on the form may be subject to criminal sanctions (including fines and imprisonment) and/or civil sanctions (including civil penalties).

Instructions to Publishers

1. Complete and file one copy of this form with your postmaster annually on or before October 1. Keep a copy of the completed form for your records.

2. In cases where the stockholder or security holder is a trustee, include in items 10 and 11 the name of the person or corporation for whom the trustee is acting. Also include the names and addresses of individuals who are stockholders who own or hold 1 percent or more of the total amount of bonds, mortgages, or other securities of the publishing corporation. In item 11, if none, check the box. Use blank sheets if more space is required.

3. Be sure to furnish all circulation information called for in item 15. Free circulation must be shown in items 15d, e, and f.

4. Item 15h., Copies not Distributed, must include (1) newsstand copies originally stated on Form 3541, and returned to the publisher, (2) estimated returns from news agents, and (3), copies for office use, leftovers, spoiled, and all other copies not distributed.

5. If the publication had Periodicals authorization as a general or requester publication, this Statement of Ownership, Management, and Circulation must be published; it must be printed in any issue in October or, if the publication is not published during October, the first issue printed after October.

6. In item 16, indicate the date of the issue in which this Statement of Ownership will be published.

7. Item 17 must be signed.

Failure to file or publish a statement of ownership may lead to suspension of Periodicals authorization.

PS Form 3526, October 1999 (Reverse)